The Att

MW01026509

Paul Foster Case

by Paul Foster Case

Copyright 2022 by Wade Coleman

June 2023 Edition

ACKNOWLEDGMENTS

Thanks to Llewellyn Worldwide for permission to use the illustrations of the Garden of Eden Before the Fall and the Garden of Eden After the Fall.

A special thanks to Carol Z for your editing.

To contact the author, write to this email.

DENDARA_ZODIAC@protonmail.com

TABLE OF CONTENTS

INTRODUCTION		4
Copyright Notice		9
CHAPTER 1	1 = 10 – Zelator	11
CHAPTER 1	Notes	69
CHAPTER 2	2 = 9 – Theoricus	71
CHAPTER 2	Notes	141
CHAPTER 3	3 = 8 – Practicus	155
CHAPTER 3	Notes	240
CHAPTER 4	4 = 8 – Philosophus	247
CHAPTER 4	Notes	324
APPENDIX 1	Ritual Notes	330
APPENDIX 2	Quadrants of a Circle	334
APPENDIX 3	Mixing Acrylic Paints	336
APPENDIX 4	Incense for Rituals	338
APPENDIX 5	Temple Furniture	340
APPENDIX 6	Winged Disk	352
PAUL FOSTER CASE BOOKS		354
WADE COLEMAN BOOKS		355

INTRODUCTION

Like the neophyte rituals, Paul Foster Case's (PFC) attunement rituals are modified Golden Dawn (GD) rituals.

Case removed most references to Greek and Egyptian gods. Also, he removed diagrams and explanations of the qlippoth.

I agree with Case that 1st Order members (and 2nd Order) should not dabble in the qlippoth and unholy creatures in general. No good comes of it. However, recall the 2 = 9 grade paper, *The Theory of Magic*.

> "The tradition of our Order admits the existence of inimical forces. They are the evil demons mentioned here and there in our rituals. Ignoring their existence is to run some risk because they impersonate beings of superhuman orders and often succeed in imposing upon the credulity of persons who ought to know better. The motive behind such impersonations appears more often to be mischief, but sometimes it seems to be a deliberate desire to obstruct human progress. There seem to be hostile powers that delight in destructiveness and disintegration. And there is abundant evidence that these powers work through human agencies. Many organizations here on Earth have directing heads consciously allied with forces they regard as evil. One of the

amazing facts of human psychology is that a relatively high level of personal intelligence and ability is by no means incompatible with a deliberate preference for anti-social objectives. They who do not admit this are simply blind to facts within the range of everyday observation. There are men and women worldwide who love evil for its own sake and devote themselves to active opposition to all that is held to be good. That such persons are the victims of delusion is true. Still, while delusion persists, the whole force of their personal activities is directed toward furthering the disintegrative processes of the universe. This is not said to frighten you. It is simply a statement of fact, verifiable by your own observation. This fact is the basis of the clause in our obligation, which binds us to use all our powers for naught but good.

Such use of powers is the best protection against inimical forces. Evil men and inimical entities have no power to injure one who practices the Magic of LVX because the entire system that goes by this name makes us a conscious agents of the benevolent forces of the universe.

To avert danger, it is necessary to be forewarned. [emphasis added] Necessary to understand what means may be employed to counteract the danger. *As in every other utilization of the forces of nature, ignorance*

constitutes the greatest danger. Fear, we are
taught, is failure; but it is perfectly possible to
exercise intelligent precaution without fear."

I offer this information not to encourage you to work with negative entities but to inform you that humanity has adversaries to our progress. Therefore, your best active defense is to perform the Lesser Banishing Ritual of the Pentagram daily.

DIAGRAMS

This print book contains black and white images. However, color books are more than double the black and white version. Therefore, you can find the colored versions in the Kindle version of this book.

When possible, color your diagrams. Coloring brings them to life and is part of the grade work. Coloring is a type of invocation and evocation.

Again, from the *Theory of Magic*,

> "Evocation is the art of calling forces which exist below human self-conscious. Sylphs, Salamanders, Gnomes and Undines are such inhabitants of the elemental kingdom, which are below that of our self-conscious awareness that humans can evoke for the purposes of LVX. Human personality has always had this relationship with sub-human powers. These powers respond to human impulses and desires automatically.

PFC describes this relationship between human and subhuman forces in his Tarot lessons on Key 8, Strength.

The *Theory of Magic* also describes invocation.

> "Invocation is accomplished by intoning these formulas [sound and color meditation with the chanting of divine names] correctly, thereby putting the consciousness of the operator in tune with the vibratory rate of these forces."

Coloring your tarot cards and grade diagrams means you spend a prolonged time looking at these symbols and imprint them deeply into your subconscious mind. In the *Fama Fraternitatis,* Brother CR indicates.

> "He did get acquaintance with those which are commonly called the Elementary Inhabitants, who revealed unto him many of their secrets."

Coloring your Tarot keys is literally and figuratively a way of making their acquaintance. And since the lower worlds reflect, the higher, the two are joined at the hip.

I offer this as a lesson and caution concerning symbols and their power.

TEMPLE DIAGRAMS

An actual temple setup varies depending on the space size and door placement. I show the temple diagrams where the different grade members are seated.

In an attunement, only the members who have obtained that grade will be allowed in the temple. For example, in a grade of Philosophus, only members that are 4 = 7 or higher are allowed to attend. In the 1 = 10 grade of Zelator, everyone except Neophytes (0 = 0) can attend.

In practice, it's all hands on deck during an attunement, so few members can sit and watch the ritual.

A member can sit in their grade position if they are not a floor officer. In our lodge, the members sat in the grade that was being attuned in order of seniority, with an empty nearest the EA for the newly attuned initiates.

Once attuned, you never leave the grade. Instead, another grade or proficiency is added.

Copyright Notice

United States Copyright Office
Library of Congress · 101 Independence Avenue SE · Washington, DC 20559-6000 · www.copyright.gov

September 29, 2021

Wade Coleman

Our reference: SR 1-10743375051

Our search in the appropriate Copyright Office indexes and catalogs that include works cataloged from 1938 through September 28, 2021 under the names B.O.T.A.; Builders of the Adytum; Paul Foster Case; F.L.O.; Fraternity of Hidden Light; and the title RITUAL OF 1=10 GRADE OF ZELATOR disclosed no separate registration for a work identified under these names and this specific title.

Our search in the appropriate Copyright Office indexes and catalogs that include works cataloged from 1938 through September 28, 2021 under the names B.O.T.A.; Builders of the Adytum; Paul Foster Case; F.L.O.; Fraternity of Hidden Light; and the title RITUAL OF 2=9 GRADE OF THEORICUS disclosed no separate registration for a work identified under these names and this specific title.

Our search in the appropriate Copyright Office indexes and catalogs that include works cataloged from 1938 through September 28, 2021 under the names B.O.T.A.; Builders of the Adytum; Paul Foster Case; F.L.O.; Fraternity of Hidden Light; and the title RITUAL OF 3=8 GRADE OF PRACTICUS disclosed no separate registration for a work identified under these names and this specific title.

Our search in the appropriate Copyright Office indexes and catalogs that include works cataloged from 1938 through September 28, 2021 under the names B.O.T.A.; Builders of the Adytum; Paul Foster Case; F.L.O.; Fraternity of Hidden Light; and the title RITUAL OF 4=7 GRADE OF PHILOSOPHUS disclosed no separate registration for a work identified under these names and this specific title.

FLOOR OFFICERS

I used abbreviations for the names of the Paul Case lodge officers. Some officer names are apparent. Others are a bit cryptic.

Paul Case	Golden Dawn
EA	Hierophant
A-n	Herius
A-t	Hegemon
H-r	Kerux
C-n	Dadouchos
P-r	Stolistes

Chiefs	
Paul Case	Golden Dawn
Pr-l	Praemonstrator
I-r	Imperator
C-n	Cancellerius

CHAPTER 1

1 = 10 RITUAL

GRADE OF ZELATOR

Golden Dawn (GD) and the Paul Foster Case (PFC) Practicus Ritual are similar. There is minor editing of the speeches and some deletions of the PFC ritual.

If I find an image online, it's included. Otherwise, I omit them.

OPENING OUTLINE

0=0 OPENING (Short Form)

1=10 OPENING

THE SIGNS OF ZELATOR

PURIFICATION AND CONSECRATION

PURPOSE OF THE WORK

ADORATION

INVOCATION

DECLARATION

END OF OPENING

1ST POINT & OPENING

ADMISSION

NEOPHYTE SIGNS AND TOKENS

OBLIGATION

PURIFICATION AND CONSECRATION

EA's ADDRESS

THE THREE PATHS

    The Path of Evil

    The Path of Good

    The Straight and Narrow Way

EA's LECTURE

    Baldric of the Zelator

    Presentation of the Cross Inside a Circle

    The Portals

    The Flaming Sword Diagram

    Altar Appointments

    Earth Tablet

    Badge – Hermetic Cross

END OF 1st POINT

2ND POINT

ZELATOR CEREMONY

ADMISSION

THE HOLY PLACE

ALTAR OF BURNT OFFERING

    Consecration with Fire

LAVER OF BRASS

    Purification by Water

THE HOLY PLACE

    Table of Shewbread Diagram

    Seven Branched Candlestick Diagram

    Altar of Incense

    The Tree Mothers Diagram

MYSTIC TITLE

    Peregrinos/Peregrine de Faustis and the symbol of Aretz.

PROCLAMATION

THE 10th PATH OF MALKUTH

    END OF ADVANCEMENT

CLOSING

ADORATION

THE PRAYER OF THE GNOMES

LICENSE TO DEPART – GNOMES

ZELATOR CLOSING DECLARATION

0=0 CLOSING (Short Form)

END OF CEREMONY

Differences Between the

PFC and Golden Dawn Rituals

OPENING RITUAL

The PFC ritual opens in the Neophyte Grade by declaration. Then the ceremony proceeds to open in the Zelator Grade.

1ST POINT

Paul Case does not use the Enochian Earth Tablet. Instead, Hebrew is used to derive an entirely different tablet. Therefore the Secret Names and King of the North are different.

2ND POINT

The EA LECTURE is similar in the two rituals. The PFC rituals offer more explanation while omitting most of the first paragraph in the Golden Dawn ritual.[1]

The SHEWBREAD and SEVEN BRANCHED CANDLESTICK lectures are similar but with slight differences. The THREE MOTHERS are unique to the PFC ritual.

CLOSING

The Secret Names and King of the North are different in the two rituals because GD uses Enochian, and PFC uses Hebrew as the basis of the Earth Tablet.

REQUIREMENTS FOR OPENING
AND 1ST POINT
IN THE GRADE OF ZELATOR

REGALIA

CHIEFS

PG with scepter, lamen, and violet mantle.

Pr-l with Scepter of Unity, lamen and blue mantle.

I-r with Scepter of Pentalpha, lamen, and red mantle.

C-s with Scepter of Reconciliation, lamen, and yellow mantle.

OFFICERS

EA with Scepter of Dominion, lamen, and red mantle.

A-n with the sword, lamen, and black mantle.

A-t with Scepter of Equilibration, lamen, and white mantle.

H-r with lamen, lamp and staff.

C-n with lamen, censer and incense.

P-r with lamen and the cup of Water

All 1=10 and above are clothed with white robes, aprons, and baldricks.

OPENING & 1ST POINT

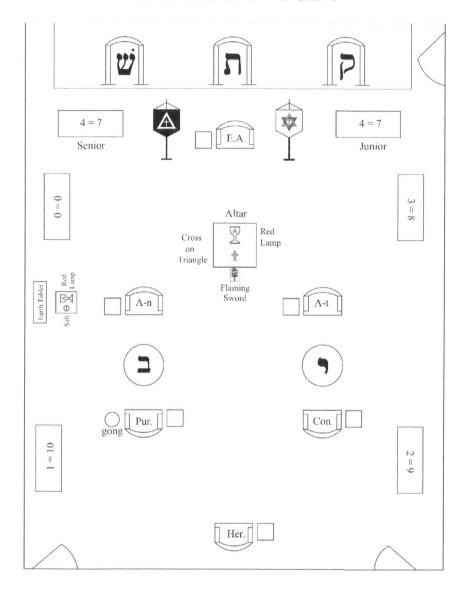

TEMPLE SETUP

EAST

EA is facing west, table at the right hand.

Banner of East at EA's left.

Banner of West at EA's right.

Portals for the 32nd, 31st and 29th Paths as shown in the diagram.

SOUTH

A-t is facing west, table at the right hand. C-n is in the southwest, facing east, table at the right hand.

WEST

H-r is facing east.

NORTH

A-n is facing west, table at the right hand.

P-r is in the northwest, facing east, table at the right hand.

Tablet of Earth on the music stand with black drape. A table before the tablet holds a red lamp on the east and a paten of salt on the west side.

PILLARS

The Pillars are placed as close to the altar as permissible. The white pillar (ʻ) is in the south. The black pillar is in the (ב) north. There's just enough room in front of the pillars for the A-n and A-t to maneuver.

ALTAR

The altar is placed as shown. Altar cloth as in 0=0 grade. On top of the altar is the Red Lamp to the east and the cross on top of the triangle to the west.

A poster-sized Flaming Sword Diagram rests on the altar's west side.

Also, place the Hermetic cross and hoodwink on the altar.

BANNERS

Banner of East to the EA's left.

Banner of West to the EA's right.

ADDITIONAL INSTRUCTIONS

During the ceremony, members not holding office will remain in their place. Only officers move from their stations during the ceremony.

Pedestal and table mean the same. Generally, the Masonic lodges have pedestals at the stations that are heavy and ornate. Our lodge supplemented these pedestals with folding TV trays for the diagrams.

Words in **bold** are chanted.

ADVANCEMENT REQUIREMENTS

ADMISSION BADGE

Hermetic cross, one for each candidate.

HOODWINK

One for each candidate.

1 = 10 BALDRIC

One for each candidate.

Standing Bell – Bowl Gong

Our temple standing bell (or bowl gong) was 18 inches in diameter and filled the temple with its note. It's a necessity for the PFC Equinox and the Zelator Ritual.

PORTALS/PATHS

Portals for the 32nd, 31st and 29th Paths as shown in the diagram below.

TABLETS

Tablet of Earth in North on a music stand, covered with a black drape.

Paten of Salt and Red Lamp on a pedestal before Tablet of Earth placed as shown above.

Since the Elemental Tablets need to be upright, music stands work best.

RITUAL OF 1=10 GRADE OF ZELATOR

0=0 OPENING (Short Form)

All: *Wait outside the temple.*

EA: *Before the Opening, after the temple has been arranged, the EA closes the door and inspects the temple. When all is in order, the EA opens the door, strikes the doorpost with one rap of his/her scepter and says:*

EA: * Fellow Initiates, take your stations and places.

EA goes to the throne and remains standing, facing west.

All: *A-n enters first, followed by A-t, H-r, C-n, P-r and Zelators. All go to their stations and places and remain standing.*

EA: Be seated. (*All sit.*) (Frater/Soror)_____, perform the Lesser Banishing Ritual of the Pentagram. (*Done*)

EA: *** *(Turns with the sun to face east.)*

All.   *Rise and face east.*

EA: *(Raising scepter aloft)*   Hidden Forces of that Limitless Light which establisheth the boundaries of the Universe, we invoke ye by the all-powerful name of your Creator *(pause)* to seal in just orientation the inner limits of this temple. May the secret virtue of the radiant east be conferred this day upon the throne of the Adept of this Temple, who is the emblem of that Dawning Light which shall illuminate the paths of the unknown and shall guide us to the attainment of the Quintessence, the Stone of the Wise, perfect Wisdom and true Happiness.

All.   So may it be! *(All face as usual.)*

EA: Dispensing with all further ceremony, I now declare _____ Lodge, No.__, open in the Grade of Neophyte!

EA: *

A-n: *

A-t: *   *(All remain standing.)*

22

1=10 OPENING

EA: * Fratres et Sorores of the (*name of organization*) _____, assist me in opening this temple in the 1=10 Grade of Zelator. (Frater/Soror) H-r, see that the temple is properly guarded.

H-r: *Goes to door, opens the door, and if there be no Sentinel, fastens door of the antechamber, then returns to the temple, closes Temple door, returns to the station, knocks and says:*

H-r: * Very Honored, Eminent Adept, the temple is properly guarded.

THE SIGNS

EA: Honored A-n, see that none below the Grade of Zelator are present.

A-n: *(Still facing West)* Fratres et Sorores, give the sign of Zelator.

All.   *All turn towards A-t, give the sign and maintain this position until the A-n and EA exchange signs.*

A-n: *(Faces east and says:)* Very Honored Eminent Adept . . . *(gives the sign to the EA, who returns it, and continues:)* . . . all present have been so honored.

EA: *Sits.*

All: *Sit.*

23

PURIFICATION AND CONSECRATION

EA: Let the Temple be purified by Water and consecrated with Fire.

Ofc: *H-r, P-r, and C-n rise and advance to the center of the temple. H-r advances to a point between the Pillars. P-r advances via the North of Black Pillar. C-n advances via the South of White Pillar. The three advance together and stop at the centerline, facing east. They give the sign of the grade.*

P-r: *Sprinkles toward the East only, saying:*

I purify by Water.

C-n: *Censes toward the East only, saying:*

I consecrate with Fire.

H-r: *(Raising staff:)* The Temple is cleansed and consecrated.

Ofc: *P-r, c-n and H-r return to stations and sit.*

PURPOSE OF THE WORK

EA: (Frater/Soror) A-t, name the element to which this grade is attributed so that it may be awakened in the sphere of this temple and the spheres of those present.

A-t: *(Remains seated)* The Element of Earth.

EA: (Frater/Soror) _____, perform the Lesser Invoking Pentagram Ritual for Earth.

(EA designates a member to perform the ritual.)

EA: Honored A-n, of what influence is this grade the sphere?

A-n: The influence of the Elements

(Optional: Astral Temple meditation by EA)

EA: (Frater/Soror) A-t, to what path is the Grade of Zelator attributed?

A-t: To the 10th Path of Malkuth, the Kingdom or Bride.

EA: Honored A-n, what power do we build in this grade?

A-n: With the power of the Resplendent Intelligence, seated in Guph, the physical vehicle of Man, operating through the balanced disposition of the Four Elements, under the dominion of the all-pervading influence of Spirit.

EA: * * * *(Rises)*

All. *All rise and face east.*

EA: Let us adore the Lord and King of Earth.

ADORATION [1]

EA: **ADONAI HA-ARETZ, ADONAI MELEK!** Unto Thee be the Kingdom, the Strength, and the Splendor! To the east, EA *makes a cross ✝ in the air with scepter.*

Malkuth, Geburah, Gedulah, the Rose of Sharon and the Lily of the Valley . . .

(makes a circle in the air with a scepter)

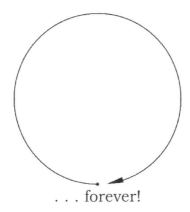

. . . forever!

All.   **AMEN.** *(All give the sign of Zelator.)*

H-r: *Goes to the North, faces North in front of the Tablet of Earth. Picks up Paten of Salt, holds on high and says:*

H-r: Let the Earth Adore Adonai!

Lowers Paten sprinkles a little salt toward the North and replaces the Paten on the pedestal.

INVOCATION

Ofc.   *All officers now go to the North, where they form*
        in front of the Tablet of Earth as follows:

EA

A-n   A-t

H-r

P-r   C-n

All.   *(All face North.)*

EA: *Unveils   Earth   Tablet.   Makes   the   following*
        invoking circle and pentagrams in the air in front
        of the Earth Tablet using his/her scepter.

EA: And Elohim said: "Let us make Adam in our
        image, after our likeness, and let them have
        dominion over the fish in the sea, and over the
        fowl of the air, and over the cattle, and over all the
        Earth, and over every creeping thing that
        creepeth upon the Earth." And the Elohim
        created Eth ha-Adam in their own image, in the
        image of the Elohim created them, male and
        female created them!

In the name of **ADONAI MELEK,** and of the Bride and Queen of the Kingdom, Spirits of Earth adore Adonai!

EA hands his/her scepter to H-r *and takes* A-n's *sword.*

In the name of **AURIEL,** the great Archangel of Earth, and in the sign of the Head of the Ox...

Traces the sign of Taurus in the center of the pentagram with the sword before the Tablet,

...Spirits of Earth adore Adonai!

(EA returns the sword to A-n *and takes* A-t's *scepter)*

In the names and letters of the Great Northern Quadrangle[2]

Makes cross + *with* A-t's *scepter in the air before the Tablet),* Spirits of Earth, adore Adonai!

EA returns the scepter to A-t *and takes the cup from Purifier.*

In the three great secret names of God, borne upon the Banner of the North: **M_ _ __O, D_ _ _ _A, V_ _ _ _ _ _ _ A** (*sprinkles toward the North*), Spirits of Earth, adore Adonai!

EA returns the cup to P-r and takes the censer from C-n.

In the name **P_ _ _ _ _ _ _ _ _ _A**, Great King of the North (*censes toward the North*), Spirits of Earth, adore Adonai!

EA returns the censer and takes their scepter from the H-r. Officers now return to their places.

All: *All face as usual and remain standing.*

DECLARATION

EA: In the name **ADONAI HA-ARETZ**, I declare that this temple is opened in the 1=10 Grade of Zelator.

EA: *** **** ***

A-n: *** **** ***

A-t: *** **** ***

END OF OPENING

1st POINT

All: *Temple arranged as in Opening for First Point. Members present, clothed with robes, aprons and baldricks. All are seated.*

EA: Fratres et Sorores, our (Frater/Soror)____, having made such progress in the paths of Occult Science as has enabled him/her to pass the examination in the requisite knowledge, is now eligible for advancement to this grade, and I have duly received a Dispensation from the Chiefs of our Order to advance (him/her) in due form. (Frater/Soror) A-t, superintend the preparation of the neophyte and give the customary alarm.

ADMISSION

A-t: *Rises and salutes EA with the Grade sign. Takes the Hermetic cross and hoodwink from the altar and leaves the temple, closing the portal behind him/her. The neophyte, robed and wearing his/her apron, is in meditation. A-t places the Hermetic cross in his/her right hand, saying:*

A-t: This is the Hermetic cross. It is your admission badge into the Temple of Malkuth, the Kingdom of the Bride.

A-t places hoodwink on the neophyte and lead him/her to the portal. A-t gives the alarm at the door and says:

A-t: *** **** *** Let me enter the Portal of Wisdom.

H-r: *H-r, carrying staff but not the lamp, opens the door and admits them.*

EA: Except Adonai build the house, they labor in vain who build it! Except Adonai keep the city, the watchman waketh but in vain! (Frater/Soror)_____ by what aid dost thou seek advancement to the 1=10 Grade of Zelator?

Neo.   *(Prompted by A-t)* By the guidance of Adonai /
By the possession of the requisite occult knowledge. /
By dispensation from the Chiefs. /
By the secret signs and tokens of a Neophyte, / and by the symbol of the Hermetic Cross.

A-t: *A-t holds up the right hand of the neophyte.*

H-r: *Then H-r takes the cross.*

NEOPHYTE SIGNS AND TOKENS

EA: Give me the step and sign of a neophyte. *(Done)*

EA: (Frater/Soror) H-r, receive from the neophyte the grip and password of the 0=0 grade.

H-r: *Receives grip and password from the neophyte, salutes EA and says:*

Very Honored, Eminent Adept, I have received them in due form.

OBLIGATION

EA: Conduct the Neophyte to a place between the Mystic Pillars.

H-r: *Places Neophyte between the Pillars, facing east.*

EA: (Frater/Soror) _____, do you solemnly promise to maintain the same strict silence regarding the mysteries of this grade which you have already sworn to maintain, respecting those of the Grade of Neophyte, never to reveal them to a Neophyte of this Order, without due dispensation from higher powers?

Neo. I do!

EA: Then you will kneel on both your knees, place your right hand on the ground and say: "I swear by the Earth whereon I kneel." *(Done)*

EA: Let the hoodwink be removed.

A-t: *A-t removes hoodwink and returns to his/her station, first cautioning the neophyte to maintain a kneeling position with the right hand on the ground.*

H-r: *While the above occurs, H-r goes North and removes Paten of Salt and takes it to the neophyte.*

EA: Take, with your left hand, a few grains of Salt now presented to you by the H-r.

H-r: *H-r presents Salt to Neophyte.*

EA: Scatter them toward the North.

H-r: *H-r indicates proper direction, and the neophyte does as told.*

EA: Say after Me: "Let the powers of Earth witness my pledge." *(Done)*

H-r: *H-r returns Paten of Salt before the Tablet of Earth and returns to assume the direction of the neophyte.*

PURIFICATION AND CONSECRATION

EA: Let the Neophyte rise. *(Done)* (Frater/Soror) Purifier and (Frater/Soror) Consecrator, purify and consecrate the Neophyte by Water and with Fire, in confirmation of (his/her) pledge.

P-r: *Purifier comes forward, left of Black Pillar and goes to the neophyte.*

C-n: *(Consecrator comes forward around White Pillar and goes to the neophyte.)*

P-r: (Frater/Soror)_____, I purify thee by Water!

Signs Neophyte as in the Mystic Repast. P-r returns to the station by the way s/he came and remains standing.

C-n: (Frater/Soror) _____, I consecrate thee with Fire!

Returns to station by the way s/he came.

P-r/C-n: *Both sit.*

EA's ADDRESS [2]

EA: (Frater/Soror) _____, I congratulate you on your perseverance in acquiring occult knowledge and passing your examination for promotion to the Grade of Zelator. Let me, therefore, point out to you that the Grade of Neophyte is merely preparatory to the others which succeed it, being, as it were, the threshold and entrance to the rest, and that its symbolism is intended to show the Hidden Light of Occult Science dawning in the darkness of the material universe. Having made sufficient progress, you are to endeavor to analyze and comprehend the nature of that light. Therefore, you now stand between the Mystic Pillars, where the secrets of the Neophyte Grade were communicated to you. *(Pause)*

Prepare to enter the Immeasurable Region!

P-r: *(Gong)*

EA: And Tetragrammaton Elohim planted a garden in Eden toward the east. And out of the ground, Tetragrammaton Elohim made to grow every pleasant tree unto the sight and good for food; the Tree of Life, also, in the midst of the garden, and the Tree of Knowledge of Good and Evil. This is the tree which hath two paths, and it is the tenth Sephirah, Malkuth, and it hath about it the seven columns, and the four Splendors whirl about it, as in the fourfold vision of the chariot of Ezekiel. From Gedulah or Chesed, it derives an influx of Mercy, and from Geburah, an influx of Severity; and the Tree of Knowledge of Good and Evil shall it be until it is united unto the Supernal Da'ath.

THE THREE PATHS

EA: But the good under it is called the angel Metatron, and the evil the angel Samael; between them lies the straight and narrow way, which is kept by the angel Sandalphon. And above it, the souls and the angels have place; beneath it, the Qlippoth or demons abide.

Let the neophyte enter the Path of Evil!

THE PATH OF EVIL [3]

H-r: *Leads Neophyte outside Pillars by the North, toward the seat of A-n.*

A-n: *Rising, threatens neophyte with the sword and says:*

Whence comest thou?

H-r: *(Prompts Neophyte)* I come from between the two Pillars / and I seek the Hidden Knowledge / in the name of Adonai!

A-n: And the angel Samael answered and said: "I am the Prince of Darkness and Evil. The wicked and rebellious man gazeth upon the face of nature and findeth therein naught but terror and obscurity. It is but darkness of darkness to him, and he is as a drunken man groping in darkness.

Points to the direction they approached.

Return, for thou canst not pass by! *(Sits)*

H-r: *H-r leads the neophyte back to place between the Pillars.*

THE PATH OF GOOD

EA: Let the Neophyte enter the Path of Good.

H-r: *H-r leads neophyte outside of the Pillars by the South, towards the seat of the A-t.*

A-t: *Rises and threatens the neophyte with a scepter and says:*

Whence comest thou?

H-r: *(Prompts Neophyte)* I come from between the two Pillars / and I seek the Hidden Knowledge / in the name of Adonai!

A-t: The great angel Metatron answered and said: "I am the Angel of the Presence Divine. The wise man gazeth upon the material universe and beholdeth therein the luminous image of its Creator. Not as yet canst thou bear the fullness of that Light.

Points to the direction they approached.

Return, for thou canst not pass by! *(sits)*

H-r: *H-r conducts neophyte back between the Pillars as before.*

THE STRAIGHT AND NARROW WAY

EA: Let the Neophyte advance by the Straight and Narrow Path, which declineth neither to the right nor left.

EA comes in front of the altar, facing west.

H-r: *H-r leads the neophyte up the center of the temple toward the altar.*

A-n/A-t:

When the candidate is between the two pillars, both officers come forward and threaten the neophyte, as before, one on the left front, the other on his/her right front, saying together:

A-n/A-t: Whence comest thou?

H-r: *(Prompts Neophyte)* I come from between the two Pillars / and I seek the Hidden Knowledge / in the name of Adonai!

EA/A-n/A-t:

EA comes forward to the West of the Altar. The EA positions the candidate so he/she is between the two pillars. EA then extends the scepter toward the neophyte's forehead. A-n and the A-t cross points of sword and scepter about the EA's scepter.

EA: But the great angel Sandalphon spake and said: "I am the Reconciler for Earth and the Soul of the Celestial therein; equally in a form invisible, in thick darkness or in blinding light. I am the left-hand Kerub of the Ark, and the Feminine Power, as Metatron is the right-hand Kerub and the Masculine; and I am the Preparer of the Pathway unto the Light Divine."

EA/A-n/A-t:

EA breaks formation, separating the insignia of the A-n and A-t. These two officers then step back: The A-n steps to the North of the Altar, facing South; the A-t steps to the South of the Altar, facing North.

H-r: *Returns to the station and sits.*

EA: *Takes neophyte by the right hand, giving grip of the First Order silently. Then draw the candidate within a few feet of the altar, points toward the Diagram of the Flaming Sword in front of the altar, and say:*

And Tetragrammaton Elohim placed a Flaming Sword at the East of the Garden of Eden, which turned every way to keep the Way of the Tree of Life.

I have much pleasure in now conferring upon you the secret signs and tokens of the Grade of Zelator. They consist of a step, a sign, a grip or token, a recognition sign, a mystic number and a password formed thereon.

THE SIGNS AND TOKENS OF ZELATOR

The step is thus given: Advance your left foot as in the Neophyte Grade, then advance the right foot before it about six inches, thus completing the pace of both feet and showing that you have crossed the threshold. In this position, extend your right arm, with your hand open, palm upward, at an angle of 45 degrees to your front. This refers to my position when I interposed between you and the Guardians of the Paths. It is the Sign of the Grade.

The Grip or Token is given thus: Lock the fingertips, as in the Neophyte Grade, then place the ball of your thumb on the knuckle of my middle finger, after which I complete the grip by placing my thumb in a similar position. The person who gives the grip always places his or her thumb in position first. This distinguishing Grip of the First Order refers to the ten Sephiroth.

The Recognition Symbol is given thus: *(Demonstrates)* It is made with the left hand and may be traced on the back of another person's hand as when giving a handshake or traced in the air before that person. It should never be given flippantly or indiscriminately, but only when there is a strong reason for believing that you are in the presence of another initiate.

The Grand Word of eight letters is Adonai Ha-Aretz, which means "The Lord of Earth," to which element this grade particularly refers.

The Mystic Number is 55, and from it is derived the password of the grade, which is Kaph-Lamed-Heh, Kallah, meaning "The Bride." It is to be lettered separately when given, the one who gives the word pronouncing the name of the first letter, the one who receives it the name of the second letter, and the one who gives it the name of the third letter, together with the pronunciation of the complete word.

BALDRIC OF THE ZELATOR

The Distinguishing Badge of this Grade, which you will henceforth be entitled to wear is the sash of the First Order, worn thus:

Puts sash on Frater/Soror and adjusts it appropriately.

This grade bears a red cross within a white triangle, and the numbers 1 and 10, also red, within a circle and a square, respectively, left and right of the triangle's apex.

JEWEL OF THE ORDER

Shows the Neophyte the Circle Cross, gives a few examples of its meaning and places it on the neophyte.

THE PORTALS

EA: The Three Portals facing you in the east represent the gates of the Paths which conduct to the Inner, leading to three other Grades, which, with those of Zelator and Neophyte, form the first and lowest Order of our Fraternity. They are the gates of the Paths of Wisdom, connecting the 10th Sephirah, Malkuth, with the other Sephiroth. The letters Qoph, Tav, and Shin, by which they are distinguished, may be arranged to make the word, Qesheth (קשת) the Bow. This bow speeds the arrow of aspiration and the Rainbow of Promise, stretched above the Earth.

THE FLAMING SWORD

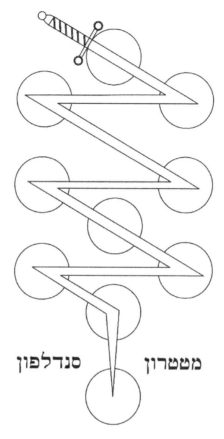

סנדלפון   מטטרון

EA: The Drawing of the Flaming Sword of the Kerubim is a diagram of the ten Sephiroth, also known as the Lightning Flash, and shows the primary descent of the Holy Influence, Mezla (מזלא), through the ten Sephiroth.

ALTAR APPOINTMENTS

In this grade, you will observe that the red cross is placed within the white triangle on the altar. The triangle refers to the three Paths connecting Malkuth with the other Sephiroth, while the cross is the Hidden Knowledge of the Divine Nature, which is to be obtained through their aid. The cross and the triangle together represent Life and Light.

EARTH TABLET

ו	ת	ל	א	י	ש	כ	ל	א	נ	ה	ל
נ	נ	א	י	ד	מ	ד	כ	ר	י	ו	א
א	ל	א	י	ק	מ	ס	ל	א	י	ל	י
ו	ר	א	ו	ט	ר	כ	ש	ש	ת	א	ל
ר	א	ל	ה	ל	ו	ת	ב	י	ל	א	מ
ה	י	ו	ג	ב	ו	ר	ר	י	ש	י	ד
מ	ד	י	ד	פ	א	כ	ו	ל	ל	ס	ל
ס	א	א	י	ו	ר	צ	ש	ת	א	ס	א
נ	ל	ל	א	ר	ל	א	כ	פ	י	ת	ר
י	ל	כ	פ	ר	א	י	מ	נ	ז	ט	ו
נ	ס	ש	ו	י	ע	י	ה	א	ר	ו	מ
מ	ל	ר	א	ס	ג	ד	ל	ע	י	ט	ס
נ	ח	ר	א	י	ר	א	י	ד	י	ה	א

This grade is specially referred to as the Element of Earth, and therefore the Great Terrestrial Tablet of the North forms one of its principal emblems.

(EA points with scepter to the Tablet in the North).

It is known as the third or Great Northern Quadrangle or Tablet of Earth, and it is one of four great Tablets of the elements. It is divided into four lesser angles, each containing a cross. The mystic letters are written in the alphabet peculiar to this grade. They represent various Divine and Angelic Names. From it are drawn the three Holy Names of God: M___o, D____a, V_____a, and numberless names of archangels, angels and spirits of all kinds which belong to the element of Earth.

H-r: *Hands Hermetic Cross to EA.*

HERMETIC CROSS

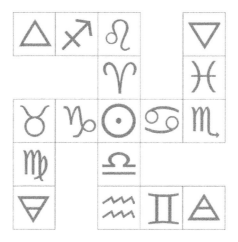

EA: You will observe that the Hermetic Cross, which is also known by the names of Fylfot Cross, the Hammer of Thor, the Swastika Cross, and the Talisman of the Jains, is formed from seventeen squares, taken from a square of twenty-five squares. These seventeen squares fitly represent the sun, the four elements and the twelve signs of the zodiac.

You will now quit the temple for a short time to meditate on what you have already learned. Your reception ceremony in the Second Point of this Grade will proceed upon your return. (*EA returns to his/her station and sits.*)

H-r: *Conducts neophyte back to the preparation room. A-t accompanies them and, while the temple is being arranged for the Second Point, makes sure the neophyte is perfect in the Grip, Sign and Password. When this is done, A-t returns to his/her station in the temple.*

END OF 1st POINT

2nd POINT & CLOSING

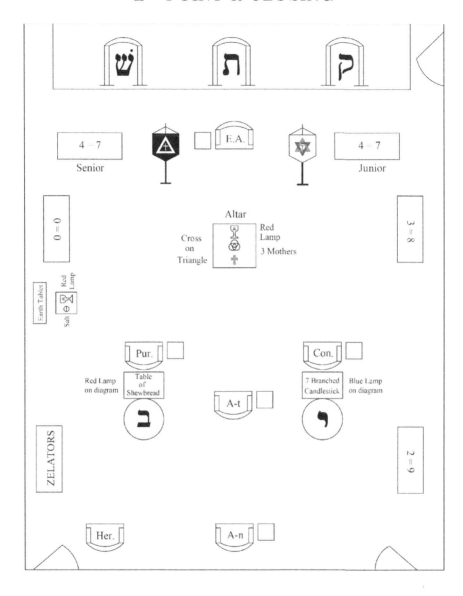

CHANGES FOR 2ND POINT

TEMPLE

Officers change positions as in the diagram. All officers, except EA, face east.

PILLARS

They are slightly west of their positions in the First Point, midway between the center of the temple and the western boundary.

ALTAR

Same as First Point, except the Diagram of Three Mothers placed in the center of the altar between the red lamp and cross and triangle.

DIAGRAMS

The diagram of Flaming Sword is removed. A diagram of the Table of Shewbread is placed on a pedestal East of the Black Pillar, Red Lamp in the center of the diagram. Diagram of Seven Branched Candlestick on a pedestal east of the White Pillar, Blue Lamp on the center of the diagram.

2nd POINT

ZELATOR CEREMONY

ADMISSION

EA: (Frater/Soror) H-r, you have my command to admit the neophyte on (his/her), giving the proper alarm. (Frater/Soror) Purifier and (Frater/Soror) Consecrator assist the H-r in the reception.

P-r/C-n: *Go to the door. Purifier stands within the temple, north of the portal. The consecrator stands within the temple, south of the portal.*

H-r: *Goes to door with Purifier and Consecrator and leaves the temple to instruct the neophyte to give the alarm of:*

*** **** ***.

H-r: Returns to the temple and stands facing the door between the P-r and C-n.

Neo: *(Gives the alarm:)*   *** **** ***

H-r: *(Admits the Neophyte, then closes the door.)*

EA: (Frater/Soror) _____, as in the Grade of Neophyte, you came from the outer world into the Porchway or entrance to the World of Occult Science, so now the progress you have made admits you to further knowledge. The Grade of Neophyte represents the Portal of the Temple, and the Grade of Zelator admits you into the Holy Place.

49

ALTAR OF BURNT OFFERING

EA: Without the door of Tabernacle or entrance to the Holy Place stood the Altar of Burnt Offering, whereon were offered the sacrifice of animals, which symbolized the Qlippoth or evil demons, which inhabit the plane contiguous to that of the Material Universe.

C-n: *Comes forward and censes neophyte in silence. The Consecrator then returns to the station and remains standing.*

LAVER OF BRASS

EA: Between the Altar of Burnt Offering and the entrance into the Holy Place stood the Laver of Brass, wherein the priests washed before entering the Tabernacle. It was a symbol of the Waters of Creation.

P-r: *Comes forward and signs the Neophyte with Water as in the Mystic Repast. After doing this in silence, he/she returns to his/her station.*

P-r:/C-n: *Both sit.*

THE HOLY PLACE

EA: Having passed the Altar of Burnt Offering and the Laver of Brass, the priest entered the Holy Place.

H-r: *Conducts neophyte to a point west of the Pillars, on the central line between North and South of the Temple. The neophyte faced east.*

A-n: *Goes East around Black Pillar and stands between the Pillars, facing neophyte and menacing him/her with Sword, and says:*

A-n: Thou canst not pass the Pillars without giving the signs, grip and password of a Neophyte. *(Done)*

H-r: *Conducts Neophyte between the Pillars to a point farther east.*

A-n: *A-n returns to his/her station through the South, passing East and South of White Pillar. Sits.*

A-t: *Rises before A-n moves and challenges Neophyte between the Pillars, with Scepter as A-n moves away, and says:*

A-t: Thou canst not enter the Holy Place without giving the signs and grip of a Zelator. *(Done)*

H-r: *Leaves neophyte and returns to his/her station and sits.*

A-t: *Tells Neophyte to follow and conducts him/her toward the Table of Shewbread and stands facing North.*

TABLE OF SHEWBREAD

A-t: On the Northern side of the Holy Place stood the Table of Shewbread. The symbolic drawing of the Rose of Creation represents its occult meaning.

Twelve small circles show the twelve signs of the zodiac. The small triangle in each circle is also the alchemical symbol of the element to which a particular sign belongs. On the left side of each triangle is the permutation of the Divine Tetragrammaton, which is peculiar to that sign.

On the right side is one of the 12 Single Letters of the Hebrew alphabet attributed to that sign. The third word in each circle is the Hebrew name of the sign. Besides representing the elemental attributes of the signs, these small triangles also allude to the division of every sign into three decans of ten degrees.

The four large triangles whose 12 angles each touch one of the 12 circles are Fire, Earth, Air and Water. They refer to the Four Triplicities of the Zodiacal Signs. In each angle of these large triangles is the name of the Tribe of Israel corresponding to that sign.

The four smaller circles near the center of the figure contain the names of the Four Archangels: Michael, Gabriel, Auriel and Raphael. A letter of the Tetragrammaton is also attributed to each circle, inscribed in the alphabet of this grade, known as the Malachim, or Writing of the Angels.

The Pentagram in the center represents the letter Heh, a symbol of the Bride of the Qabalistic Microprosopus and the alchemical Queen. The lamp at the center symbolizes the Sun, the source of light and heat. The lamp's base rests on the Pentagram because the physical radiance and energy of the Sun are but outer manifestations of a spiritual power which, from time immemorial, has been represented by the five-pointed star.

The whole figure is a synthesis of the visible Universe. Furthermore, the twelve circles represent the twelve foundations of the Holy City described in Revelation. The Christian symbolism of the Pentagram is referred to as Christ, and the star of twelve rays formed by the large triangles represents the twelve Apostles.

A-t: *Leaves neophyte, returns to his/her station, and sits.*

SEVEN BRANCHED CANDLESTICK

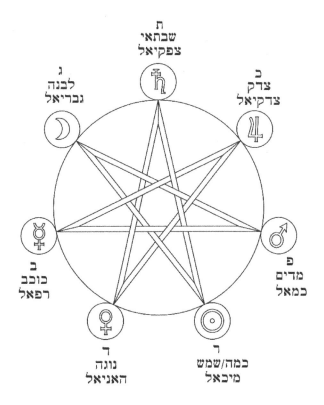

A-n: *Comes forward and conducts neophyte to the South, facing the Diagram of the Seven Branch Candlestick, and says:*

A-n: On the Southern side of the Holy Place stood the Seven-Branched Candlestick. The symbolic drawing before you represents its occult meaning.

The seven circles surrounding the Heptagram represent the seven planets and the Qabalistic Palaces of Assiah. This material world answers to the seven apocalyptic churches in Asia or Assiah, as these again allude to the seven lamps of fire before the throne on a higher plane.

Each circle is shown in the planetary color in the King Scale of color attributions. In addition, within each circle is the symbol corresponding to the heavenly body assigned to that circle.

Outside each circle is one of the Seven Double Hebrew letters assigned to the corresponding planet or luminary, together with the Hebrew name of each and the name of the angel governing it.

The Heptagram itself alludes to the Seven Days of the week and shows how their order is derived from that of the Seven Planets when placed at the seven angles of the Heptagram. The Heptagram's rays bear the circles' colors whence they proceed.

Within the small heptagon at the center of the Heptagram is the Shield of David, or Star of Love, also the Star of the Macrocosm. Upon it is placed a blue lamp, representing the Astral Light of the Universe, formed into a focus by the Seven Interior Stars corresponding to the Seven Spheres.

As the Seven Golden Candlesticks of the Apocalypse answer to the Seven Planetary spheres, so do the seven stars of the same vision refer to the Seven Archangels which rule them: for the seven stars are angels of the Seven Churches, and the Seven Candlesticks which thou sawest are the Seven Churches.

A-n returns to the seat and sits.

ALTAR OF INCENSE

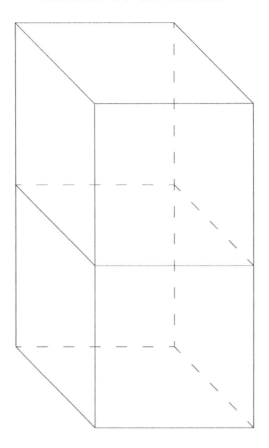

EA: *Comes forward and conducts Neophyte to West of Altar. EA puts the scepter on the altar, takes the censer from the Consecrator and then censes before the altar with three swings and says:*

Within the Mystic Veil, which separated the Holy of Holies from the Holy Place, stood the Ark of the Covenant. Before the Veil stood the Altar of Incense, of which the altar now before you is a symbolic representation. It was in the form of a double cube, thus representing material form as the reflection and duplication of that which is spiritual. Together with the top and underside, the altar's sides consist of ten squares, thus symbolizing the ten Sephiroth. The basal one will be Malkuth, the realization of the rest upon the Material plane and the others are concealed behind. For were this double cube raised in the air before your head, you would see but the single square forming the lowest side, the others from that position being concealed from you; just so behind the Material Universe lies the concealed form of The Majesty of God.

The Altar of Incense was overlaid with Gold to represent the highest degree of Purity, but the altar before you is black to represent the Terrestrial Earth. Learn thus to separate the pure from the impure, the refined and spiritual Gold of the Alchemists from the Black Dragon of Putrefaction and evil.

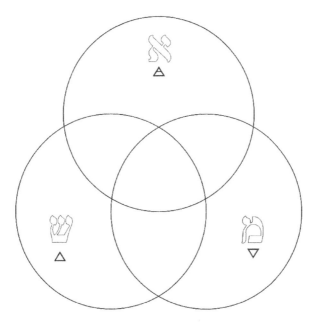

EA: Upon the Cubical Altar were Fire, Water and Incense. These are symbolized by the three circles in the diagram on the altar. The interlaced circles stand for the Three Primal Elements. The yellow circle represents the Element of Air and bears the Mother letter Aleph (א), attributed to that element. The blue circle, representing Water, bears the letter Mem (מ), attributed to that element. Finally, Shin (ש) and the red circle symbolize the element of Fire.

The interlacing of these three circles produces the primary colors' blending to form the secondary colors: green, orange, and violet. By various mixtures, these secondary colors produce the Citrine, Russet, Olive and Black of the Sephirah Malkuth, shown at the center of the diagram. The white circle containing a red fire triangle symbolizes spiritual light concentrated in the energy of universal fire.

The geometrical proportions of this figure are such that they combine the relations necessary to describe the two great magical symbols, the Hexagram and the Pentagram. According to the Queen Scale, the colors show the attributions of the Sun, Moon, and the Five Planets to the Ancients.

Thus the diagram is a synthesis of the most important fundamentals of our work. Mark it well, and use it often, following the special instruction you will receive from the C-s.

The meaning of the cross within the triangle was explained in the First Point.

EA: I now congratulate you on having attained the Grade of Zelator, and in recognition thereof, I confer upon you the Mystic Title of (Peregrinos/Peregrine) de Faustis. It signifies that you are still far from the goal reached by perfected Adepts. I also give you the symbol of Aretz (ארץ), which is Hebrew for Earth.

The word Zelator is said by some to be derived from the Egyptian "Zal Athor," signifying "Searcher of Nature." Still, others assign it the meaning of "Zealous Student," whose first duty is to blow the fire beneath the Alchemist's Crucible. *(Returns to his/her throne and sits.)*

H-r: *Conducts newly admitted Zelator to their seat in the temple.*

H-r returns to his/her station.

EA: * (Frater/Soror) H-r, you have my command to proclaim that this neophyte has been advanced to the Grade of Zelator.

PROCLAMATION

H-r: *Coming to EA's right front, as usual, says:*

In the Name of Adonai and by command of the Eminent Adept, hear ye all! I proclaim that (Frater/Soror)____, having made sufficient progress in the study of Occult Science, has been duly advanced to the Grade of Zelator and that (he/she) has received the Mystic Title of (Peregrinos/Peregrine) de Faustis and the symbol of Aretz.

Returns to station and sits.

THE 10th PATH OF MALKUTH

EA: In the Grade of Zelator, the mystic symbolism of the Tenth Sephirah, Malkuth, is shown, with which this grade is especially connected, as well as the tenth Path of the Sepher Yetzirah, or Book of Formation.

Among its mystic titles, Malkuth has that of Sha'ar (שער), "The Gate," which by metathesis makes Osher (עשר), or "Ten." It is also called in Chaldaic, Throa (תרעא), "The Gate," which has the same number as Adonai, fully written by its letters Aleph-Daleth-Nun-Yod, which both equal 671 by numeration.

It is also called "The Gate of Tears," "The Gate of Death," "The Gate of the Shadow of Death," "The Gate of Justice," "The Gate of Prayer," and "The Gate of the Daughter of the Mighty One." It is also the Gate of the Garden of Eden and the Inferior Mother; Christian symbolism connects it with the three holy women at the foot of the cross.

The tenth Path of the Sepher Yetzirah, which answereth unto Malkuth, is called the Resplendent Intelligence because it is exalted above every head and sitteth on the Throne of Binah. It illuminateth the splendor of all the lights and causes the current of the Divine Influx to descend from the Prince of Countenances, the great angel Metatron.

(Frater/Soror) _____, before you are eligible for advancement to the next higher grade of the order, you must have been a member of this grade for at least six months. You must also make yourself perfect in the subjects contained in the Knowledge Lecture of the Grade of Zelator. When you are thoroughly and genuinely perfect, you will signify the same by letter to the C-s, and arrangements will be made for your examination.

END OF ADVANCEMENT

CLOSING

EA: * Fratres et Sorores of the _____, (*name of organization*) assist me in closing this temple in the Grade of Zelator. (Frater/Soror) H-r, see that the temple is properly guarded.

H-r: *Goes to door, as in Opening, checks the outer door, returns to the temple and closes the portal. Returns to station and says:*

    * Very Honored Eminent Adept, the temple is properly guarded.

ADORATION

EA: *** *(All rise)* Let us adore the Lord and King of Earth.

All: *(Face East)*

EA: **ADONAI HA-ARETZ, ADONAI MELEK!** Blessed be Thy Name unto the endless ages!

All: **AMEN.** *(All give the sign of the grade.)*

THE PRAYER OF THE GNOMES

Ofc: *The Officers go North and form as in Opening. H-r conducts the new Zelator to the North and places him/her between the A-t and A-n. All others face North.*

(Earth Tablet in the North)

EA

A-n   Zel   A-t

H-r

P-r   C-n

EA: Let us rehearse the Prayer of the Gnomes or Earth Spirits.

O Invisible King of all things! Thou who has taken the Earth for Thy footstool and excavated abysses therein to fill them with Thine Almighty power! Thou whose name maketh the vaults of the Universe tremble! Thou who causest the seven metals to flow in their veins of stone! Monarch of the Seven Lights! Remunerator of the subterranean workers! Lead us, we pray Thee, unto the desirable Air and unto the Kingdom of Light! We watch, and we labor without cessation. We seek and hope for Thee by the twelve stones of the Holy City, the talismans concealed therein, and the axis of lodestone traversing the center of the Earth.

O Lord! O Lord! O Lord! Have pity on those who suffer. Expand our hearts, detach and elevate our minds, and enlarge our entire being.

O thou who are the equilibrium of stability and movement! O Day enveloped in Night! O darkness, clothed with Brilliance! O thou, our Master, who never keepest back unto Thyself the wages of Thy workman! O Silver Whiteness! O Golden Glory. O Crown of living and harmonious diamonds! O thou who wearest the heavens on Thy finger like a sapphire ring, thou who hides beneath the Earth in the Kingdom of stone, the marvelous seed of stars, live, reign and be the Eternal Dispenser of the riches of which Thou hast made us the guardian.

LICENSE TO DEPART - GNOMES

EA: *Makes the following banishing Pentagrams and circle in the air in front of the Tablet using his/her scepter, and says:*

Depart ye in peace unto your habitations. May the blessing of **ADONAI** rest with you. Be there peace between you and us, and be ready to come when ye are called.

EA: *   *(EA veils Earth Tablet.)*

All: *Return to their places and face as usual and sit.*

EA: Frater/Soror _____, perform the Lesser Banishing Pentagram of EARTH.

The designated member performs the Lesser Banishing Ritual of the Pentagram.

DECLARATION

EA: In the name of **ADONAI HA-ARETZ,** I declare this temple closed in the Grade of Zelator.

EA: *** **** ***

A-n: *** **** ***

A-t: *** **** ***

0=0 CLOSING (Short Form)

EA: Dispensing with all ceremony, I now declare this temple closed as a Hall of Neophytes.

EA: *
A-n: *
A-t: *

END OF CEREMONY

CHAPTER 1 NOTES

[1] TRACING THE EQUAL-ARMED CROSS

The cross is drawn with the lines traced on top of each other. The lines are shown below with separation to emphasize the directions – start in the center, trace top to bottom, back to center, then right to the left.

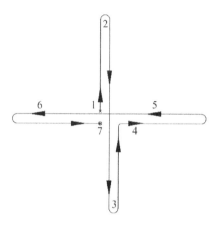

[2] EA's ADDRESS

This was deleted in the PFC ritual: "For He has created nature that man being cast out of Eden may not fall into the Void. He has bound man with the stars with a chain. He allures him with Scattered Fragments of the Divine Body in bird and beast and flower, and He laments over him in the Wind and in the Sea and in the birds. When the times are ended, He will call the Kerubim from the East of the Garden, and all shall be consumed and become Infinite and Holy. Receive now the secrets of this grade."

[3] MENACING THE CANDIDATE

Do not threaten the candidate with the sword by pointing the tip at them. It is best to present the flat of the blade for safety reasons. For example, you can trip, or the candidate can take a step forward, and you can stab them if you are not careful.

[4] BETWEEN THE PILLARS

At the beginning of the ritual, it says, "Prepare to enter the Immeasurable Region!" In this astral realm, the candidate meets the guardians. Afterward, the candidate is placed between the pillars. Then the EA, with the grip of the 1st Order, leads the candidate to the altar, where they receive instruction. Therefore, minimizing the distance between the pillars and the altar is best to emphasize this symbolic point.

CHAPTER 2

2 = 9 RITUAL

GRADE OF THEORICUS

Golden Dawn (GD) and the Paul Foster Case (PFC) Theoricus Ritual are similar. However, there are deletions in the speeches in the PFC ritual.

Case rewrote the Four Element Purification section in the Path of Tav. He removed Egyptian God imagery and replaced it with the Tree of Life.

If I find an image online, it's included at the end of the chapter notes. Otherwise, I omit them.

OPENING OUTLINE

0=0 OPENING (Short Form)

2=9 OPENING

THE SIGNS OF THEORICUS

PURPOSE OF THE WORK

ADORATION

INVOCATION

DECLARATION

END OF OPENING

71

1ST POINT

ADMISSION

ZELATOR SIGNS AND TOKENS

OBLIGATION

32nd PATH OF TAV (ת)

      SOUTH Gate – Purification with FIRE

      WEST Gate – Purification by WATER

      EAST Gate – Purification by AIR

      NORTH Gate – Purification by EARTH

EA's ADDRESS

EA's LECTURE

      Key 21

      Garden of Eden – Holy City

      4 Seas, 7 Earths and 7 Infernal Mansions

MYSTIC TITLE

      Lord/Lady of the 32nd Path

END OF 1st POINT

2ND POINT

THEORICUS CEREMONY

RECEPTION

LECTURE – THE 32nd PATH OF TAV

    Badge – Caduceus of Hermes

    Serpent of Wisdom

    Altar Appointments

    Theoricus Signs and Tokens

    The Portals

    Tablet of Air

    Kamea of the Moon

    Magic Line of the Moon

    Moon on the Tre of Life

    Cube of Space

    Lineal Figures

    Beryl

    Geomatic Figures

MYSTIC TITLE

    Poraios/Poraia de Rejectis & symbol of Ruach.

PROCLAMATION

EA'S ADDRESS

      END OF ADVANCEMENT

CLOSING

ADORATION

THE PRAYER OF THE SYLPHS

LICENSE TO DEPART – SYLPHS

    Lesser Banishing Pentagram of AIR

THEORICUS CLOSING DECLARATION

0=0 CLOSING (Short Form)

    END OF CEREMONY

Differences Between the

PFC and Golden Dawn Rituals

The GD ritual explicitly declares, "The Temple opened in the Grade of Theoricus." The PFC ritual implies the opening.

The PFC ritual adds chanting to the PURPOSE OF THE WORK.

In the DECLARATION, the GD ritual uses a battery of 9 knocks of three, each 3-3-3. In the PFC ritual, it's 2-3-4.

In the PATH OF TAV, the speeches of the four guardians are different because the PFC ritual omits sections. Also, the order of the directions is different.

The Secret Names and King of the North differ in the two rituals because GD uses Enochian, and PFC uses Hebrew as the basis of the Air Tablet.

Also, in the ADORATION, the PFC ritual omits the italic letters shown below. "In the Names and letters of the Great Eastern Quadrangle *revealed unto Enoch by the Angel Ave*, Spirits of Air, adore your Creator."

1ST POINT

FOUR ELEMENT PURFICATION

The order of the Four Elements of Purification are different. In the GD ritual, the candidate carries the Banner of the East and displays it to the East (Air) and South (Fire) guardians – active elements. Then the candidate carries the West Banner for the directions West (Water) and North (Earth) – passive elements.

The order of procession in the PFC ritual is South – West – East – North. I don't know why.

In the PFC ritual, the candidate carries the Cubical Cross for the entire purification in their right hand. In their left hand, they carry the implement of the officer leading them around the temple.

The four officers are described as Egyptian Gods in the GD ritual, while the PFC ritual uses the Tree of Life and planetary imagery.

Direction	Case	Golden Dawn
East	Venus & Netzach	Hormakhu, rising Sun
West	Jupiter & Chesed	Toum, the setting Sun
North	Saturn & Binah	Khephra, Sun at Night
South	Sun & Tiphareth	Ra, (Sun at Noon)

Since the imagery is different, this section was entirely rewritten by Case.

2ND POINT and CLOSING

THE PATH OF TAV

The CADUCEUS OF HERMES lecture is moved to a grade paper in the PFC ritual.

The ALTAR APPOINTMENTS[6] section is so different I included the GD version in the Chapter Notes.

The lecture on beryl is unique to the PFC ritual.

The TABLETS OF AIR are different. GD uses Enochian, and the PFC tablet is derived from Hebrew.

REQUIREMENTS FOR OPENING AND

1st POINT IN

THE GRADE 2 = 9 THEORICUS

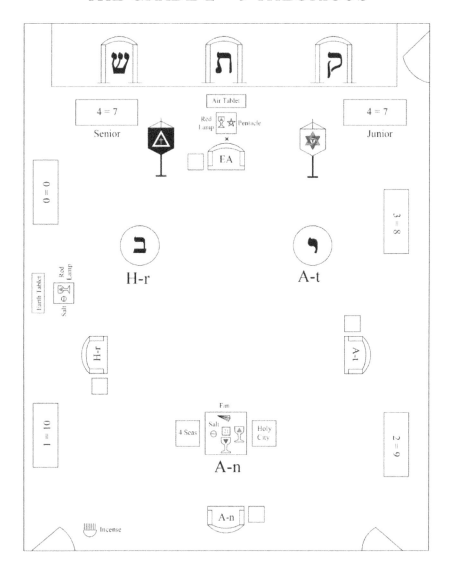

REGALIA

CHIEFS

PG with scepter, lamen, and violet mantle.

Pr-l with Scepter of Unity, lamen and blue mantle.

I-r with Scepter of Pentalpha, lamen, and red mantle.

C-s with Scepter of Reconciliation, lamen, and yellow mantle.

OFFICERS

EA with Scepter of Dominion, lamen, and red mantle.

A-n with the sword, lamen, and black mantle.

A-t with Scepter of Equilibration, lamen, and white mantle.

H-r with lamen, lamp and staff.

C-n with lamen, censer and incense.

P-r with lamen and the cup of Water

All 1=10 and above are clothed with white robes, aprons and baldricks.

TEMPLE SETUP

EAST

Station of the EA with a table at the right. Tablet of Air on a music stand with a yellow drape above and behind the throne, below the Portals.

SOUTH

Station of A-t with a table at the right.

WEST

Station of A-n with a table at the right.

NORTH

H-r with a pedestal at the right hand. Above and behind is the Tablet of Earth on a music stand with a black drape.

PILLARS

The pillars are placed as shown in the diagram. White pillar (') south, black pillar (ב) north.

ALTAR

Placed halfway between the center of the temple and the station of the A-n. Altar cloth as in Neophyte Grade. Centered on top of the altar is Key 21. East of Key 21 is a fan. South is a red lamp. West of Key 21 is a cup. North is a paten of salt.

BANNERS

Banner of the East to the EA's left.
Banner of West to the EA's right.

ADVANCEMENT REQUIREMENTS

ADMISSION BADGE

Cubical Cross of 22 Squares.

HOODWINK

One for each candidate.

2 = 9 BALDRIC

One for each candidate.

DIAGRAMS

A table to the south of the altar for the Diagram of Eden. The Diagram of Four Seas is on a table on the north side. Tarot Key 21 on the Altar.

PORTALS/PATHS

Above and behind the throne of the EA, the Hebrew letters Shin (ש), Tav (ת), and Qoph (ק), as in 1=10.

PEDESTALS/TABLES

One for each officer (4). One each for the Earth and Air Tablets (2). One on each side of the altar (2). 8 total.

When storage space is an issue, folding TV trays work best.

TABLETS

NORTH

Tablet of Earth, black-draped, on a music stand. A table before the tablet holds a red lamp on the east and a paten on the west.

EAST

Air Tablet, yellow-draped, on a music stand. A table before the tablet holds a red lamp on its north and a pentacle on the south.

There should be sufficient space between the pedestal and the throne to permit the EA to stand facing the tablet, holding the Pentacle with arms fully extended.

ADDITIONAL INSTRUCTIONS

During the opening ceremony in the Grade of Theoricus, members not holding office never leave their places. Only officers move from their stations. When there is no advancement, meetings of this grade are held in a Temple arranged for the second point because all members have attained the full grade.

Words in **bold** are chanted.

RITUAL OF 2=9 GRADE OF THEORICUS

0=0 OPENING (Short Form)

All: *Wait outside the temple.*

EA: *Before the Opening, after the temple has been arranged, the EA closes the door and inspects the temple. When all is in order, the EA opens the door, strikes the doorpost with one rap of his/her scepter and says:*

EA: * Fellow Initiates, take your stations and places.

     EA goes to the throne and remains standing, facing west.

All: *A-n enters first, followed by A-t, H-r and Theorici. All go to their stations and places and remain standing.*

EA: Be seated. (*All sit.*)   (Frater/Soror)_____, perform the Lesser Banishing Ritual of the Pentagram of Earth. (*Done*)

EA: *** *(Turns with the sun to face East.)*

All: *(Rise and face East)*

EA: *(Raising scepter aloft)*   Hidden Forces of that Limitless Light which establisheth the boundaries of the universe, we invoke ye by the all-powerful Name of your Creator *(pause)* to seal in just orientation the inner limits of this temple. May the secret virtue of the radiant East be conferred this day upon the throne of the Adept of this Temple, who is the emblem of that Dawning Light which shall illuminate the paths of the unknown and shall guide us to the attainment of the Quintessence, the Stone of the Wise, perfect Wisdom and true Happiness.

All: So may it be! *(All face as usual.)*

EA: Dispensing with all further ceremony, I now declare _____ Lodge, No.__, open in the Grade of Neophyte!

EA: *

A-n: *

A-t: *
      (All remain standing.)

2=9 OPENING

EA: * * * Fratres et Sorores of the (*name of organization*) _____, assist me to establish this Temple in the Grade of Theoricus. (Frater/ Soror) H-r, see that the temple is properly guarded.

H-r: *Salutes with Grade sign. Takes staff, leaves lamp at their station. Goes to the door, as usual. On re-entering the temple, the H-r knocks once, *, on the inner side of the door, striking with the black end of the staff. Then returns to the station, faces EA, salutes again and says:*

Very Honored, Eminent Adept, the temple is properly guarded.

Remains standing at station.

THE SIGNS

EA: Honored A-n, see that none below the Grade of Theoricus be present.

A-n: Fratres et Sorores give the sign of Theoricus.

All: *All but EA and A-n give the sign.*

A-n: Very Honored Eminent Adept, . . . *(A-n gives the sign and EA answers.)* . . . the lives of all present rest on the Foundation of Eternity.

All: *EA sits. All sit.*

PURPOSE OF THE WORK

EA: (Frater/Soror) A-t, name the element to which this grade is attributed so that it may be awakened in the sphere of this temple and in the sphere of those who are present.

A-t: The Element of Air.

EA or 2nd Order member performs the Lesser Invoking Pentagram Ritual of Air.

EA: Honored A-n, of what influence is this Grade the Sphere?

A-n: The influence of the Moon.

(Optional: Guided meditation by EA)

EA: (Frater/Soror) H-r, what path did you attain to this grade?

H-r: Through the 32nd path of the letter Tav, ascending from Malkuth.

EA: (Frater/Soror) A-t, to what does the 32nd path allude?

A-t: To the Universe, composed of the Four Elements; to the Kerubim; to the Qlippoth; to the Astral Plane; to the Fire of the Serpent-power; to the planet Saturn; to the Temple of Holiness in the midst, supporting all things; and to the Cross of Service.

EA: Honored (Frater/Soror) A-n, to what path is the Grade of Theoricus attributed?

A-n: To the 9th Path of Yesod, the Basis or Foundation.

EA: (Frater/Soror) H-r, with what power do we build in this grade?

H-r: With the power of the Purified Intelligence, seated in Nephesh, the Animal Soul of Man, energized by the Serpent-fire of Saturn.

EA: * * *

All: *All rise.*

(Cantor sounds the tone E. The six intonations following are all on the same pitch.)

EA: **BEFORE ALL WORLDS,**

All: **I WAS;**

A-n: **IN ALL WORLDS,**

All: **I AM;**

A-t: **AND WHEN WORLDS ARE BUT A MEMORY,**

All: **I SHALL BE.**

EA: Let us adore the Lord and King of Air.
(Faces East.)

All: *Face East.*

ADORATION

EA: **SHADDAI EL CHAI**, Almighty and Ever-living, by Thy Name, magnified in the life of all.

All: **AMEN**. *(All give the sign of grade.)*

INVOCATION [1]

Ofc: *Air Tablet is unveiled by EA and Earth Tablet by H-r. EA returns to the original place but faces East. A-n moves eastward through the middle line of the temple to a point just west of the altar. At the same time, A-t and H-r move diagonally from their stations to positions just West of the Pillars. In these positions, they face East: The A-t West of the White Pillar, the H-r west of the Black Pillar.*

EA: *With the scepter, makes the following invoking circle and pentagrams before the Air Tablet:*

EA: And the Elohim said: "Let us make Adam in our image, after our likeness, and let them have dominion over the fowl of the air." In the Name **YOD HEH VAV HEH**, and in the Name **SHADDAI EL CHAI**, Spirits of Air, adore your Creator!

Up to this point, EA stands west of his/her throne. Now places the scepter on the pedestal at the right hand of the throne and goes behind the throne to a position directly west of the Tablet of Air. Takes Pentacle in right hand and says:

EA: In the Name **RAPHAEL**, great Archangel of Air, and in the sign of Man, ♒ *(makes the sign of Aquarius in the air before the Tablet with Pentacle),* Spirits of Air, adore your Creator!

In the names and letters of the Great Eastern Quadrangle[2]...

(makes ✝ with Pentacle before the tablet),

...Spirits of Air, adore your Creator!

(Holding Pentacle on high) In the Three Secret Names of God, borne on the Banner of the East, **N_ _ _ _I, M_ _ _ CHE, T_ _ _ _ _ _ _CHE**, Spirits of Air, adore your Creator!

Still holding the Pentacle on high, says:

In the Name
R_ _ _ _ _ _ _ _ _ _ _ _CH, great King of the Air, Spirits of Air, adore your Creator! *(Replaces Pentacle. Returns to the throne and takes scepter.)*

Ofc: *Officers return to their stations.*

All: *All face as usual but remain standing.*

89

DECLARATION

EA: In the Name **SHADDAI EL CHAI**, I declare this temple to be established in the Temple of Holiness by the power of the Purified Intelligence, energized by the Serpent-fire of Saturn.

EA: * * * * * * * * *

A-n: * * * * * * * * *

A-t: * * * * * * * * *

EA: *Sits.*

All: *All sit.*

END OF OPENING

EA: Fratres et Sorores, our (Frater/Soror)_____ *(Aspiration Name)*, having passed the examination in the requisite knowledge, is now eligible for advancement to the Grade of Theoricus, and I have received a Dispensation from the Prolocutor to advance (him/her) in due form. (Frater/Soror) A-t, superintend the preparation of the Zelator and give the customary alarm.

A-t: *Salutes and leaves the temple. Prepares the Zelator, who is robed and wearing the apron and Baldric of 1=10. A-t gives him/her the Cubical Cross, to be held in his/her right hand, and says:*

This is the Cubical Cross[3]. It is your admission badge into the Path of Saturn, the Assisting Intelligence.

Zelator is then hoodwinked and led to the portal. A-t knocks with the battery of the grade.

H-r: Places Fan from Altar at the right hand of EA;
      Lamp at the right hand of A-t;
      Cup at the right hand of A-n;
      the paten of salt at the right hand of H-r.

      This done, H-r goes to the portal and knocks
      once on its inner side, using the black end of the
      staff. This informs the A-t the temple is
      prepared:

H-r: * Remains standing near the portal.

ADMISSION

A-t: Knocks on portal: * *   * * *   * * * *
      Takes Zelator by the right elbow to lead him/her.

H-r: Admits them and closes the portal after them.

A-t/
Can: Advances about three steps into the temple, stops
      and faces East.

A-t: Quit the Material, and seek the Spiritual.

H-r: Comes to Zelator's left side. A-t and H-r conduct
      the Zelator, moving with the Sun, around the
      temple to a point just west of the pillars,
      between them, and facing the East. Takes
      Cubical Cross from Zelator.

EA: Give the step of Zelator. (*Done*)
Give the sign of Zelator. (*Done*)
Give the recognition sign of the First Order. (*Done*)
(Frater/Soror) A-t, receive the grip or token from the Zelator and the Grand Word of the Grade of Zelator.

A-t: (Frater/Soror)____ *(aspiration name)*, give me the grip of Zelator. *(Done)*
Give me the Grand Word. (*Done*)
Very Honored, Eminent Adept, I have received them in due form.

EA: (Frater/Soror) H-r, receive the Mystic Number of the Grade of Zelator and the Password formed thereon.

H-r: (Frater/Soror)____ (a*spiration name)*, give me the Mystic Number of Zelator. *(Done)* Give me the Password. *(Done)* Very Honored, Eminent Adept, I have received them in due form.

EA: Give me the title and symbol you received in that grade. *(Done)*

OBLIGATION

EA: (Frater Peregrinos/Soror Peregrine) de Faustis, do you solemnly pledge yourself to maintain the same strict secrecy concerning the mysteries of the 32nd Path and of the Grade of Theoricus, which you have already sworn to maintain respecting those of the preceding grade?

Can: I do.

H-r: *Returns Cubical Cross to Zelator's right hand.*

EA: Then you will stretch forth your right hand, holding the Cubical Cross toward heaven, and say: "I swear by the firmament of heaven."

Can: *Does as directed, prompted if necessary by A-t.*

EA: Let the hoodwink be removed.

A-t: *Removes hoodwink. Takes it and return to their station. H-r remains with Zelator.*

EA: Stretch forth your right hand, holding the cross toward the East, in the position of the Zelator sign, and say: Let the powers of Air witness my pledge.

Can: *Does so. H-r prompts, if necessary.*

32nd PATH of TAV (ת)

EA: Facing you are the portals of the 31st, 32nd and 29th Paths, leading from the Grade of Zelator to three other Grades, which are beyond. The only path is now open to you is the 32nd, which leads to the Grade of Theoricus. This path you must now traverse before you reach that degree. Take in your left hand the staff of the H-r.

H-r: *Places staff in Zelator's left hand.*

EA: Guided by Hermes the Guardian, enter now the path through which thou mayest pass from the Material to the Spiritual.

H-r: Hermes the Guardian, said unto the Aspirant:

> What thou seekest,
> Truly THAT thou art.
> The treasure thou journeyest afar to find
> Is the Jewel of Eternity
> In thy heart of hearts.

Conducts Zelator, through Pillars, to position before the station of the A-t.

SOUTHERN GATE

A-t: *As they approach, rises and menaces Zelator with a scepter, and says:*

Thou canst not pass the Gate of the Southern Heaven unless you tell me my name.

H-r: *(For Zelator):*
Thou art the FACE which shineth ever,
And before thee, the darkness hasteth way.
Thou art the Glory of the Eternal Source,
And the Foundation of the Kingdom of the Eternal Result.

A-t: *(Lowers scepter.)* In what signs and symbols do ye come?

H-r: In the letter Shin, with the Staff of Science and the symbol of the Cubical Cross.

PURIFICATION BY FIRE

A-t: *Hands scepter to H-r. Picks up the lamp and makes the sign of Leo before Zelator. Replaces the lamp on the pedestal.*

In the sign of the Lion, Child of Fire, thou art purified.

A-t takes the scepter back from the H-r. H-r takes staff from Zelator.

A-t: Because thou knowest me, my power is thine.

A-t places his/her scepter in Zelator's left hand and holds Zelator's left hand for a second to reinforce passing the power.

H-r: *Returns to their station, crossing the temple to do so.*

A-t: *Leaves station to conduct Zelator. They continue around the temple to a position before the station of the A-n.*

WESTERN GATE

A-n: *As they approach, rises and menaces Zelator with the sword.*

Thou canst not pass the Gate of the Western Heaven unless thou canst tell me my name.

A-t: *(For Zelator):*

Thou art the Lord of FORTUNE
Whosoever conforms his acts to thy Will
Shall know thee in truth as the Father of Mercy
Whose chariot in the heavens
Is Tzedek, the Great Benefactor.

A-n: *(Lowers sword.)* In what signs and symbols do ye come?

A-t: In the letter Mem (מ), with the Scepter of Equilibration and the symbol of the 22 letters.

PURIFICATION BY WATER

A-n: *Hands sword to A-t. Picks up the cup and, with it, traces the sign of Scorpio before Zelator. Replaces cup on the pedestal and says:*

A-n: In the sign of the Eagle, Child of Water, thou art purified.

A-n takes the sword back from the A-t.
A-t takes the scepter from the Zelator.

A-n: Because thou knowest me, my power is thine.

A-n places his/her sword in Zelator's left hand, points upward and holds Zelator's left hand for a second to reinforce passing the power.

A-t: *Returns directly to their station.*

A-n: *Leaves station to conduct Zelator. They pass through the North to a position facing the EA.*

EA: *Rises, menacing Zelator with the scepter.*

Thou canst not pass the Gate of the Eastern Heaven unless you tell me my name.

A-n: *(For Zelator):*

Thou art the portal.
Through thee Life, Eternal and Unbounded,
Entereth the realm of temporal and limited creation.

EA: *(Lowers scepter.)* In what signs and symbols do ye come?

A-n: In the letter Aleph (א), with the Sword of Justice and the symbol of Equilibrated Forces.

PURIFICATION BY AIR

EA: *Hands scepter to A-n. Picks up the fan and traces the sign of Aquarius before Zelator. Replaces fan on the pedestal and says:*

In the sign of the Man, Child of Air, thou art purified.

(EA takes the scepter back from the A-n.)

A-n: *Takes the sword from the Zelator.*

EA: Because thou knowest me, my power is thine.

EA places his/her scepter in Zelator's left hand and holds Zelator's left hand for a second to reinforce passing the power.

A-n: *Returns to their station through the center of the temple but south of the altar.*

EA: *Leaves station to conduct Zelator. They pass round the temple, by South and West, to a position facing H-r.*

NORTHERN GATE

H-r: *Rises, holding staff before Zelator, as when barring the way in the Grade of Neophyte. Does not touch Zelator but holds staff horizontally, as described, and says:*

Thou canst not pass the Gate of the Northern Heavens unless you tell me my name.

EA: *(For Zelator):*

Thou art the MOUTH whence issueth the Breath of Life;
Thou art the all-devouring one
Whereunto all things return
"Beginning and End"
Is thy holy name.

H-r: *Holding a staff in right hand only, says:*

In what signs and symbols do ye come?

EA: In the letters Shin, Mem and Aleph, and the symbols of the Scepter of Dominion and the Cross of Service.

PURIFICATION BY EARTH

H-r: *Hands staff to EA, picks up Paten of Salt, and, with it, traces the sign of Taurus before Zelator. Replaces paten on the pedestal and says:*

In the sign of the Head of the Ox, Child of the Elements, thou art purified.

H-r takes the staff back from the EA.

EA: *Takes the scepter from the Zelator.*

H-r: Because thou knowest me, my power is thine.

H-r places his/her staff in Zelator's left hand and holds Zelator's left hand for a second to reinforce passing the power.

EA: *Returns to the throne.*

H-r: *Leaves station and conducts Zelator to the East, between the pillars. Takes Cubical Cross from Zelator and hands it to EA, who then hands the H-r the fan.*

H-r/A-t./A-n:

H-r, A-t, and A-n now go to the altar. H-r carries the fan. A-t carries the lamp. A-n carries the cup. They replace these symbols in the proper positions on the altar. The three officers return to their stations. A-t and A-n sit.

H-r takes the paten of salt to the altar, places it thereon, and returns to the Zelator, between the pillars. While this is going on, the EA is speaking to the Zelator.

EA'S ADDRESS

EA: Child of the Elements, four times purified by knowledge, attend the first lesson of this grade.

The Way of Liberation leads Within. Never in the world of reflected forms surrounding thee shalt thou find the Stone of the Wise. Within thee is the treasure of treasures. The powers thou shalt learn to wield are powers of thine own Spirit. For thou art Man and Man is God's perfect image of His eternal dominion over all.

By knowledge mayest, thou find Within Thyself the balance of forces symbolized by the Scepter of Equilibration. By knowledge mayest thou learn the keen discrimination of the Sword of Justice. By knowledge mayest thou discover that humanity is truly the Scepter of Divine Dominion. By knowledge mayest thou add to knowledge and truly measure all the forces of creation by the Staff of Science.

Yet knowledge shall avail thee little if it is not joined to use. One by one, the instruments of the Magic of Light have been given thee, but as yet, thy grasp is weak. Hence they were placed in thy left hand.

As thou passed through the 32nd Path, in thy right hand was the Cubical Cross. It is a fitting emblem of the balanced forces of thy Spirit, joined together in the Cross of Service. For not otherwise, by devoted service may you gain the skill to wield the powers you have learned to know.

Therefore, the 32nd Path of Wisdom is called the Path of Assisting Intelligence. Learn from this that only by devoted service to thy fellow creature mayest thou serve Him Whose image thou art, and so come at length to the full enjoyment of the Highest Good.

Of the other meanings of this Path, thou shalt learn from the instructions given in a lecture pertaining to this grade.

H-r: *Who has been standing at Zelator's left hand, now takes staff from Zelator. Returns to their station, leaving Zelator standing between the pillars.*

EA: Now standest thou alone, O Aspirant, yet not alone, for within thee are the powers of all thy Great Companions of the Hidden Way.

Pauses then leave the throne, advances to Zelator, gives the First Order Grip, and draws Zelator toward the East from between the pillars. They go around the white pillar to the West of the Altar, facing East.

EA: The 21st Key of Tarot is a synthesis of the occult meanings of the 32nd path. Hence it is also a summary of all thou hast experienced in this ceremony. Study it well.

The fan, lamp, cup and paten of salt represent the four elements and their inhabitants, the Sylphs, Salamanders, Undines, and Gnomes.

Be thou, therefore, prompt and active as the Sylphs, but avoid frivolity and caprice. Be energetic and strong like the Salamanders, but avoid irritability and ferocity. Be flexible and attentive to images, like the Undines, but avoid idleness and changeability. Be laborious and patient, like the Gnomes, but avoid grossness and avarice. So shalt thou gradually develop the powers of thy soul and fit thyself to command the spirits of the elements.

As in the preceding grade, the altar represents the material universe, composed of the Four Elements.

Garden of Eden – Holy City [4]

A diagram representing the Garden of Eden is on its right, with the Tree of Life at the center. The same diagram also symbolizes the Holy City, the Paradise of Regeneration. The colored squares refer to the Grades of our Order.

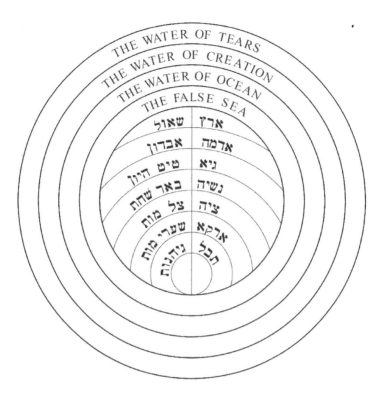

THE WATER OF TEARS
THE WATER OF CREATION
THE WATER OF OCEAN
THE FALSE SEA

שאול	ארץ
אבדון	אדמה
טיט היון	גיא
באר שחת	נשיה
צל מות	ציה
שערי מות	ארקא
גיהנם	תבל

On the left of the altar is a diagram representing the Four Seas, the Seven Earths, and the Seven Infernal Mansions which are the abodes of the Qlippoth. The Qlippoth are the Shells of the Dead, whose power is released and purified by the Magic of Light, employed in the Work of Regeneration.

A more extended explanation of the diagrams is given in a lecture pertaining to this grade.

H-r: *Leaves station and comes to the left side of the Zelator.*

MYSTIC TITLE

EA: *Returns to the throne, stands facing the Zelator, and says:*

I now have much pleasure in conferring upon you the title of (Lord/Lady) of the 32nd path.

You will now quit the temple for a short time to meditate upon what you have learned. Your reception ceremony into the Grade of Theoricus will proceed upon your return.

END OF THE 1st POINT

CHANGES FOR 2ND POINT

TEMPLE

EAST

The Kamca of Luna, the Magical Line of Luna, the Moon on the Tree of Life, and the Cube of Space diagrams are placed on TV trays, as shown in the drawing below.

SOUTH

Diagram of Lineal Figures.

WEST

Diagram of Soham (Beryl). Behind A-n's station, the Portal of Tav.

NORTH

Near H-r is the Geomantic Figures Diagram.

ADMISSION BADGE

The H-r's Caduceus lamen.

PORTALS/PATHS

Portals in the East changed to Resh, Samekh, and Tzaddi.

ALTAR

The altar is moved between the H-r and A-t stations and draped in violet. Leaning against the west side is a poster-sized Serpent of Wisdom diagram. The altar center has a white triangle, apex toward the west. On the triangle is the Red Cross of 6 Squares. North of the triangle is the cup of water, and south is a red lamp.

PILLARS

White pillar (‎ו) close to Altar on South Side.
Black Pillar (‎ב) close to Altar on North Side.

PEDESTALS/TABLES

One for each officer (4). One each for the Earth and Air Tablets (2). One for each side of the EA station (2). Lineal, Geomancy and Soham diagrams (3). 11 total.

Having separate tables for the Lineal, Geomancy and Soham diagrams is best. Otherwise, the illustrations can be placed on the officers' tables, which is awkward.

The banners are moved as well.

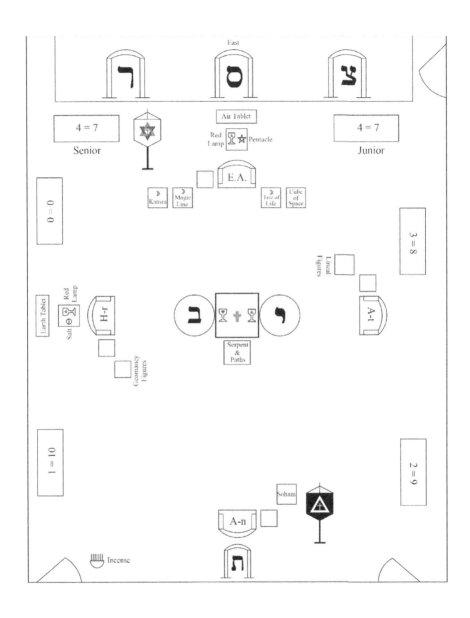

2nd POINT

THEORICUS CEREMONY

EA: * * *   (Frater/Soror) H-r, you have my command to call the Initiates to work.

H-r: * * *   Fellow Initiates, take your stations and places.

All: *All sit upon reaching their stations and places.*

EA: (Frater/Soror) H-r, instruct the Zelator in the proper alarm and present him/her with the necessary Admission Badge.

  (Frater/Soror) A-t, guard the portal and admit them when the proper alarm is given.

RECEPTION

H-r: *H-r leaves the temple. Says to Candidate.*

  This is the Caduceus of Hermes. It is your admission badge into the Temple of Yesod.

A-t: *A-t goes to the portal.*

H-r: *(H-r instructs Zelator to give alarm:*
  * *   * * *   * * * *

A-t: *A-t opens the door and leads Zelator in a little way. Faces Zelator toward the East.*

H-r: *H-r closes the door.*

EA: (Frater Peregrinos/Soror Peregrine) de Faustis, in the Zelator Grade, after having been prepared as a Neophyte, you entered this order as a prince, returned from a far country, and destined eventually to rule the kingdom to which you had been restored.

However, before exercising your birthright, you must learn the rules and practice the disciplines of mastery. This is our ancient order's true purpose and all its work and instruction.

The lesson of the 32nd path, through which you have just passed, is that a willingness and ability to serve are indispensable for mastery.

Having learned this lesson, you are now prepared to make further progress.

(Frater/Soror) A-t, conduct the Zelator to the west, facing the path of the letter Tav, by which he/she has entered this grade.

H-r: *Returns to their station.*

A-t: *Conducts Zelator to West, facing A-n, and points out the Portal of Tav.*

A-n: By what symbol do you enter here?

A-t: By the Caduceus of Hermes, the peculiar emblem of the H-r. *Take the Admission Badge from Zelator and give it to A-n.*

CADUCEUS OF HERMES

A-n: *Turns Admission Badge to face Zelator and says:*

A-n: The Tree of Life and the three Mother letters are keys to unlock the meaning of the Caduceus of Hermes. In a lecture pertaining to this grade, you will find this meaning explained in detail. Here it is enough to say that this Admission Badge depicts an important fact concerning the occult constitution of man. This fact bears directly upon all works of the Magic of Light.

(Lays Admission Badge aside.)

EA: *Leaves throne. Comes to the east of the Altar without the scepter.*

A-t: *Conducts Zelator to the west side of the altar. Tells Zelator to remain there. Returns to own station.*

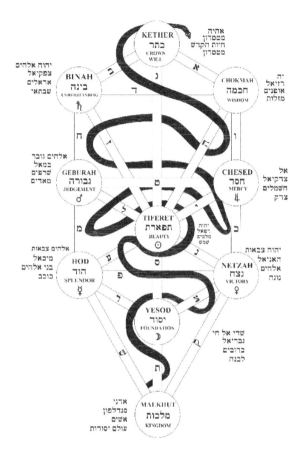

EA: Before you, as in the preceding grade, stands the Tree of Life formed of the sephiroth and their connecting paths. You saw it standing amid the Garden of Eden and the Holy City, the Paradise of Regeneration, in the First Point of your advancement. Having quit the Material, in your quest for the Spiritual, learn now that this Tree of Life diagram is like a map or chart of the inner kingdom you were created to rule. Observe particularly that the Serpent of Wisdom, as it rises, touches the paths of the 22 letters but never enters any of the 10 circles. Note also its color, the black, sometimes attributed to the planet Saturn.

Upon each sephirah are written in Hebrew letters its name, the Divine Name ruling it, and those of the Angels and Archangels attributed to it. The connecting Paths are twenty-two in number and are distinguished by the twenty-two letters of the Hebrew alphabet, making with the Ten Sephiroth themselves, the 32 Paths of Wisdom of the Sepher Yetzirah.

EA: The Cross within the Triangle, apex downward, at the center of the Altar top, is another key to the nature of the secret force employed in the Magic of Light. In that force are blended a fiery essence, symbolized by the Red Cross, and a watery substance, represented by the White Triangle.

The Red Lamp and the Cup of Water further mark these hot and moist natures.

The Altar cloth is a Cross of Five Squares. Its color, violet, is attributed to Yesod, the Foundation, and the sephirah corresponding to this grade.

Observe that in violet, the red of Fire and the blue of Water are also blended.

The pillars stand close to the altar, leaving no room for passage on either side of the altar. Only by utter sacrifice of everything material to your quest for the spiritual may you enter fully into the inheritance of Spiritual Israel, your birthright of complete dominion.

Faces East, gives the sign of Theoricus, holding the sign while sayings:

Glory be unto Thee, Lord of the Land of Life, for Thy Splendor filleth the universe.

THEORICUS SIGNS AND TOKENS

EA: *After a short pause, comes to the West of the Altar and says:*

The Grade of Theoricus is referred to as Yesod, the Basis or Foundation. As the name Theoricus intimates, the principal object of this grade is to instruct you in the fundamental theory upon which your practice of the Magic of Light must be based. To this grade, certain signs and tokens are attributed. They consist of a Sign, Token, Grand Word, Mystic Number and Password formed therefrom.

The sign is given thus: stand with feet together and raise both arms upward and back, palms up as if supporting a weight. It represents you in the Path of Yesod, supporting the pillars of Mercy and Severity. In relation to the Magic of Light, it is symbolic of the truth that the Spirit, which you really are, is the sole support of the world you are destined to govern.

The grip or token is that of the First Order, which you received in the preceding grade.

The Grand Word is a Name of seven Hebrew letters, Shaddai El Chai, which means "The Almighty of Life."

The Mystic Number is 45, and from it is formed the Password, which is Mem (מ) Heh (ה), Mah (מה), the Secret Name of the World of Formation. It is to be lettered separately when given, the one who gives the word pronouncing the first letter, the one who receives it the second, and the one who gives it pronouncing the Secret Name.

The Ninth Path of Wisdom is attributed to this grade and the Sephirah Yesod. It is called Purified Intelligence.

I most earnestly commend you for giving your most serious attention to the occult meaning of this path, as expounded in one of the lectures of this grade. There you will find the basis of theory indispensable to your success in practicing the Magic of Light.

BALDRIC OF THE ZELATOR

The Distinguishing Badge of this Grade, which you are now entitled to wear, is the Baldric of Zelator, with the addition of a violet cross above the triangle, and the numbers 2 and 9, in a circle and square, respectively, left and right. Beneath the triangle is placed the number 32, between two parallel white lines.

(EA returns to East and sits.)

A-t: *Goes to Zelator and guides him around Pillar B to the East.* Then, while the EA speaks, return to the station.

THE PORTALS

EA: The three portals facing you are the gates of Paths leading from this grade. That on your right connects with the Grade of Philosophus, that on your left with the Grade of Practicus, while the central one leads to the Portal of the Vault of the Adepts.

TABLET OF AIR

ס	ה	ר	נ	צ	א	ב	ד	ר	ו	נ	ב
י	ע	ר	ש	ת	ר	ג	ב	ו	נ	ע	י
נ	ס	י	ה	א	ל	א	נ	ס	ו	ת	ת
ד	ל	ל	נ	י	מ	ד	ל	י	א	ו	ו
ה	א	א	ז	א	ל	ח	ס	ש	ל	ר	נ
ש	י	י	א	י	ר	ו	נ	מ	ס	ע	ש
נ	ק	ג	מ	ר	א	ה	ת	ע	ר	ו	ח
י	מ	ה	מ	י	מ	ו	א	ו	א	ג	ד
א	כ	ש	נ	מ	ר	ש	א	נ	י	ר	ר
ל	צ	ל	א	י	ק	ד	ח	ל	א	מ	ג
פ	נ	ו	א	ר	ד	ו	ה	א	נ	ע	ר
ל	א	י	ר	ב	מ	א	ל	א	י	ד	ו
ה	מ	ל	א	פ	ר	ל	א	י	ר	ו	ז

EA: This Grade especially refers to the Element of Air. Therefore, the Great Watchtower, or Terrestrial Tablet of the East, forms one of its principal emblems.

EA: *Points with scepter to the tablet.*

EA: The mystic letters upon it are written in the alphabet peculiar to this grade. They represent various Divine and Angelic Names. From it are drawn the three Holy Secret Names of God;
N_ _ _ _i M_ _ _ che Th_ _ _ _ _ _che, and numberless names of archangels, angels, and spirits of all kinds, belonging to the Element of Air.

זל	חע	טכ	ע	אכ	בס	גי	דנ	ה
ו	חל	טע	ל	אע	בכ	גס	די	ומ
זמ	ז	טל	פ	אל	בע	גכ	הנ	הי
וי	חמ	ח	מ	אפ	בל	דס	דכ	ונ
זנ	זי	טמ	ט	אמ	גע	גל	הס	הכ
וכ	חנ	חי	נ	א	במ	דע	דל	וס
סז	זכ	טנ	י	אנ	ב	גמ	הע	הל
ול	חס	טי	ס	אי	בנ	ג	דמ	וע
זע	חכ	טס	כ	אס	בי	גנ	ד	מה

EA: (Conducts Zelator to Kamea of the Moon.) The Grade of Theoricus and the Sephirah Yesod corresponds to the Sphere of Influence exerted by the Moon. Before you is its Kamea, or Magic Square, composed of 81 lesser squares, or cells, containing various combinations of Hebrew letters representing the numbers from 1 to 81. Every column, vertical, diagonal, or horizontal, results in the same summation, 369, which is the number of the name of Chasmodai, Spirit of the Moon.

The sigils of Angels, Spirits and Intelligences related to the Lunar Influence are drawn from this square.

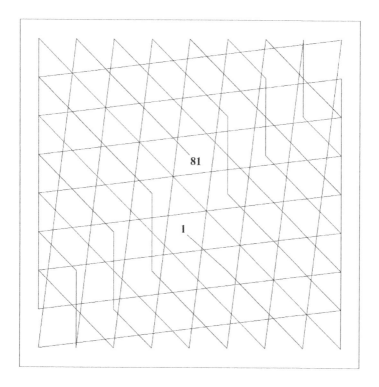

EA: *Moves Zelator to in front of the Magic Line of the Moon.*

From the Kamea is produced the Magic Line of the Moon, a continuous line drawn from center to center of the cells, beginning at the number 1 and ending at 81. The beginning of the line is marked by a crossbar and ends with an arrow point.

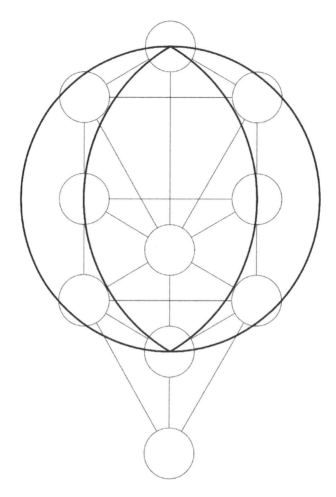

EA: *Moves Zelator to in front of the diagram of the Moon on the Tree of Life.*

Before you are shown the Lunar symbol's meaning when inscribed upon the Tree of Life. Its crescent in increase represents the side of Mercy; its crescent in decrease the side of Severity; at full, it reflects the Sun of Tiphareth.

CUBE OF SPACE

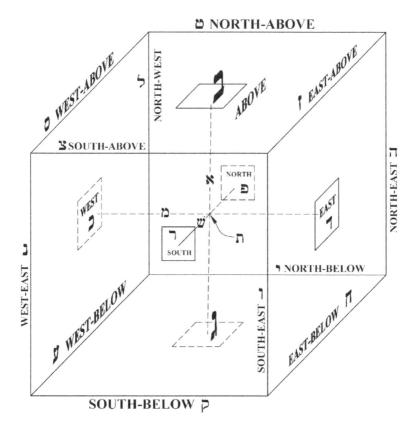

EA: *Moves Zelator to in front of Cube of Space diagram.*

The Grade of Theoricus is attained through the 32nd path of the letter Tav (ת), whose Tarot attribution, the Universe, was explained to you earlier.

An important esoteric teaching regarding the Universe is given in the Sepher Yetzirah. Before you is a resume of that teaching, in which the manifested universe is represented as a cube.

The six faces of this cube and its interior center are assigned to the seven double letters of the Hebrew alphabet. The three interior coordinates correspond to the three mother letters. The twelve boundary lines represent the twelve simple letters.

A-t: *Returns to Zelator.*

EA: *Leaves Zelator and goes to own station after A-t has arrived.*

LINEAL FIGURES

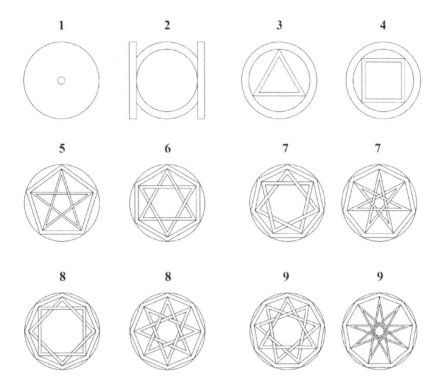

A-t: *Conducts Zelator to A-t's station in the south.*

(Frater Peregrinos/Soror Peregrine) de Faustis, the mastery of the kingdom's powers within, calls for thorough theoretical and practical knowledge of numbers and the lineal figures relating to them.

Before you is a tablet containing a selection of these figures, from the black circle with a white center corresponding to the number 1 to the figures representing the number 9.

This is not the only way these figures may be drawn and colored. The special forms chosen for this tablet have particular reference to influences active in this Grade of Theoricus.

A-n: *Leaves station and goes to Zelator.*

A-t: *Leaves Zelator and sits.*

A-n: *Guides Zelator to West.*

(Frater Peregrinos/Soror Peregrine) de Faustis, our Ancient Brethren penetrated deep into the mysteries of life without by any means exhausting those mysteries.

Their investigation continues today, and modern scientific research influenced and directed by the Third Order of our Fraternity brings to light many things that confirm and develop the findings of those who followed the Hidden Way in earlier periods of history.

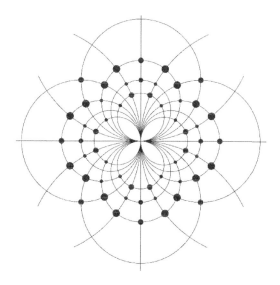

A-n: The diagram before you is one of many examples of this. It shows what human eyes had never seen until 1912 when this beautiful proof that God does truly geometrize was established by sending x-rays through a beryl crystal to impinge on a photographic plate.

Curved lines connecting certain points have been added to bring more clearly before your eyes the wonderful symmetry of the molecular structure of the crystal and its relation to the construction pattern for the diagram of the Tree of Life.

The Hebrew word Soham is what the Wise of Israel gave to the beryl. Its number is 345. This has many illuminating correspondences you will undoubtedly learn during your occult studies.

GEOMANTIC FIGURES

♄	▽	CARCER	⦂	♑	△	TRISTITIA	⦂	♒
♃	△	ACQUISITO		♐	▽	LATITIA		♓
♂	△	PUER		♈	▽	RUBEUS		♏
☉	△	FORTUNA MAJOR		♌		FORTUNA MINOR		♌
♀	△	PUELLA		♎	▽	AMISSIO		♉
☿	△	ALBUS		♊	▽	CONJUNCTIO		♍
☽	▽	POPULUS		♋	▽	VIA		♋
☊		CAPUT DRACONIS			☋	CAUDA DRACONIS		

H-r: *Leaves station and goes to Zelator.*

A-n: *Leaves Zelator and sits at their station.*

H-r: *Guides Zelator to North.*

> (Frater Peregrinos/Soror Peregrine) de Faustis, our Ancient Brethren knew, as well, that the causes of all events in human life are really internal, proceeding from the cause of causes, the Universal Intelligent Energy, which is the Source, Mover, and Knower behind all the phenomena of the manifested universe.

> Because this Universal Intelligent Energy is omnipresent, it is a real presence at any given point in space and the real presence at the heart of every human personality. That presence is the True Self and the author of all knowledge – Past, Present and Future.

Ordinarily, this perfect knowledge of the True Self is Hidden from us, but through divinatory practices, such as Geomancy, some part of it may be brought down into the personal level of awareness.

Before you are represented, the 16 figures of Geomancy, formed from all the combinations of single and double points in 4 lines, can possibly occur. Two are attributed to each of the seven planets, and the remaining two to Caput and Cauda Draconis. Some are also attributed to Fire, others to Air, and others to Earth or Water. They are also classed under the signs of the zodiac.

The meaning of the Tablet of Earth was explained to you in the Zelator Ritual.

H-r conducts Zelator to a seat in the Southwest, returns to their station in the North, and sits.

MYSTIC TITLE

EA: I now congratulate you on having attained the Grade of Theoricus, and in recognition thereof, I confer upon you the Mystic Title of (Poraios/Poraia) de Rejectis, which means "Brought from among the Rejected Ones," and I give you the symbol of Ruach, which is Hebrew for Air.

EA: (Frater/Soror) H-r, you have my command to declare this Zelator has been duly advanced to the Grade of Theoricus, (Lord/Lady) of the 32nd path, and has received the Mystic Title of (Poraios/Poraia) de Rejectis.

PROCLAMATION

H-r: *Comes to North-East, as usual, and faces west. Raises staff vertically and says:*

In the name of SHADDAI EL CHAI, and by the command of the Eminent Adept, hear ye all!

I proclaim that our (Frater/Soror)_____ *(aspiration name)*, having made sufficient progress in the study of Occult Science, has been duly advanced to the Grade of Theoricus, (Lord/Lady) of the 32nd path, and that (he/she) has received the mystic Title of (Poraios/Poraia) de Rejectis and the symbol of Ruach.

(Returns to their station and sits.)

EA'S ADDRESS

EA: Members of the 2=9 Grade may have a period of not less than six months to prepare for advancement and notify the C-s anytime after that period of their readiness to be examined by the Pr-1 or a designated representative.

END OF ATTUNEMENT

CLOSING

EA: * Fratres et Sorores of the (*name of organization*)_____, assist me in closing the temple in the Grade of Theoricus.

EA: (Frater/Soror) H-r, see that the temple is properly guarded.

H-r: *As in Opening, salute, leaves lamp at the station. Goes to the door, as usual. On re-entering the temple, the H-r knocks once, *, on the inner side of the door, striking with the black end of the staff. Then returns to the station, faces EA, salutes again and says:*

H-r: Very Honored, Eminent Adept, the temple is properly guarded.

ADORATION

EA: * * * *(All rise.)* Let us adore the Lord and King of Air.

All: *Face East.*

EA: **SHADDAI EL CHAI**, Almighty and Ever-living, blessed be Thy Name unto countless ages.

All: **AMEN**. *(All give Sign of Grade.)*

PRAYER OF THE SYLPHS

Ofc: *Officers then form as in Opening: The EA behind the throne, before the pedestal; H-r at West of Black Pillar; A-t West of White Pillar; A-n on the centerline of the temple, at a point midway between altar and station. Members in places facing East.*

EA: Let us rehearse the prayer of the Sylphs.

Spirit of Light, Spirit of Wisdom, whose breath giveth forth and withdraweth the forms of all things; Thou before whom the life of beings is but a shadow which changeth, and a vapor which passeth away; Thou Who ascendest upon the clouds, and dost fly upon the wings of the wind; Thou Who breathest forth Thy Spirit, and endless space is peopled; Thou Who drawest in Thy Breath, and all that came forth from Thee unto Thee returneth. Movement without cessation, amid Eternal Stability, be Thou blessed forever!

We praise Thee, bless Thee in the changing empire of created light of shadows, reflections and images, and aspire without ceasing toward Thine immutable and imperishable splendor. Let the ray of thine Intelligence, and the warmth of thy love, penetrate even unto us.

Then what is volatile shall be fixed, the shadow shall become a body, the breath of air shall be a soul, and the dream shall be a thought.

No longer shall we be swept away by the tempest, for we shall bridle the winged steeds of dawn and guide the evening winds to bring us into Thy Presence.

O, Spirit of Spirits! O, Eternal Soul of Souls! O, Imperishable Breath of Life! O, Creative Sigh! O, Mouth which breathest forth and withdrawest the life of all beings in the ebb and flow of Thine Eternal Word, which is the Divine Ocean of movement and truth!

All: AMEN.

EA: *Makes with scepter the following Banishing Pentagrams and Circle in the air before the Air Tablet:*

EA: Depart ye in peace unto your habitations. May the blessing of **YOD HEH VAV HEH** rest with ye. Be there peace between you and us, and be ye ready to come when ye are called. * *(EA veils Air tablet.)*

All: *Return to their places.*

H-r: *H-r veils Earth Tablet.*

EA: V.H. Frater/Soror _____, perform the Lesser Banishing Pentagram of AIR.

Designated Second-Order member or, if there be none, the EA performs the Lesser Banishing Ritual of Air.

DECLARATION

EA: In the Name of **SHADDAI EL CHAI**, I declare this temple closed in the Grade of Theoricus.

EA: * * * * * * * * *

A-n: * * * * * * * * *

A-t: * * * * * * * * *

0=0 CLOSING (Short Form)

EA: *If meetings of other grades do not follow the 2=9 Closing, then the EA proceeds to close the temple in the Grade of Neophyte, using this short form:*

Dispensing with all ceremony, I now declare this temple closed as a Hall of Neophytes of the (*name of organization*) _____.

EA: *

A-n: *

A-t: *

END OF CEREMONY

CHAPTER 2 NOTES

[1] INVOCATION

The officers form up behind the tablet for the invocation in the three other rituals.

EA

A-n   A-t

H-r

The placement of officers differs depending on the ritual, but the formation is a triangle or diamond-like. However, it is different in the 2 = 9 ritual. The EA stands behind his chair, shown as an "X" below.

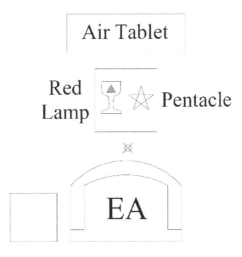

It's a tight fit since the EA is on the raised dais. The placement of the officers on the steps with the EA chair is awkward, and the reason I believe the officers do not form a diamond pattern in this ritual.

The cross is drawn with the lines traced on top of each other. The lines are shown below with separation to emphasize the directions – start in the center, trace top to bottom, back to center, then right to the left.

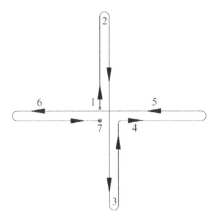

³ THE CUBICAL CROSS

The Golden Dawn and PFC cubical cross are different.

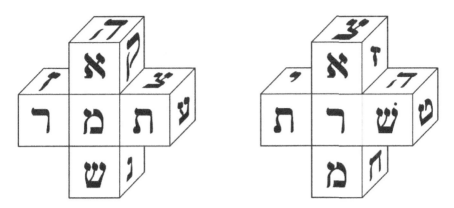

By laying the Golden Dawn cube flat, we have this image. I determined the letters on the cube's bottom from an online image. Laying the cube flat, we have this image.

By changing the letters to their astrological signs, a pattern develops.

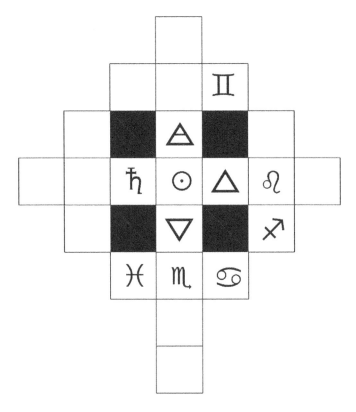

The signs are arranged by their elements. Since there is no mother letter for Earth, Saturn is the symbol.

Filling in the blanks, we have this figure.

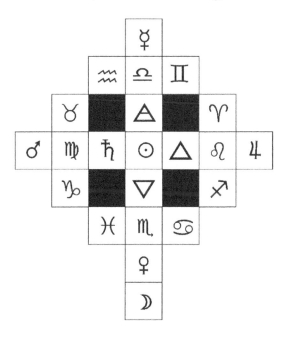

Aleph is the root of Air. The Air signs are Gemini, Libra and Aquarius. Note that Mercury is dignified by Triplicity by Day in Air signs.

Mem is the root of Water. The Water signs are Cancer, Scorpio and Pisces. Venus is dignified by Triplicity by Day in Air signs and the Moon by the common Triplicity.

Shin is the root of Fire. The Fire signs are Aries, Leo and Sagittarius. Jupiter is dignified by Triplicity by Night in Fire signs and the Sun by Day.

Earth has no mother letter; therefore, the Golden Dawn cube uses Saturn. The Earth signs are Taurus, Virgo and Capricorn. Mars is dignified by common Triplicity in Earth signs.

PFC Cube

Laying the PFC cube flat, we have this image.

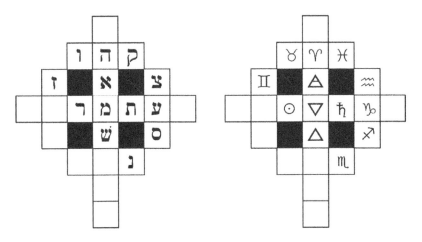

The interested student can fill in the blanks.

The GD Cubic Cross is built around the 4 elements and astrology's dignity by Triplicity.

The PFC Cross conveys the idea of the planet's progression through the twelve signs of the zodiac.

Pat Zalewsky, *Inner Order Teachings of the Golden Dawn* (p. 219-226), gives a detailed explanation of this diagram.

⁵ FOUR SEAS

7 EARTHS & 7 INFERNAL MANSIONS

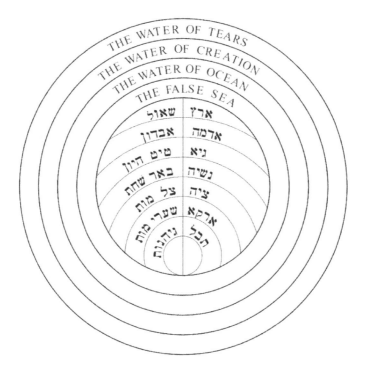

This diagram is not included in the grade work but is part of the temple diagrams. The lecture concerning the diagrams has this to say,

"The diagram of Gehenna, or the Four Seas, is not reproduced in this text. It should **NOT** be drawn by members below the Second Order. Nor should copies of it, especially colored ones, be kept in the homes of 1st Order members, for, simple as it is, this diagram easily becomes a material base for powerful forces with which tyros are unprepared to cope. In lodges, its use is attended by adequate protections."

It's always a good idea to surround ourselves with life-affirming symbols and people. And it is best to keep a safe distance from people and images of death and destruction. However, ignorance will not protect us from negative influences. Usually, the easiest path is to avoid trouble which requires us to know what it looks like.

Pat Zalewsky, *Inner Order Teachings of the Golden Dawn* (p. 227 - 238), gives a detailed explanation of this diagram with coloring instructions.

The 7 (ish) Earths

The 7 (ish) Earths			
Sephiroth			**Meaning**
Supernals	Aretz	ארץ	Earth, country. Earth of Genesis. Dry, crumbling earth.
Chesed	Adamah[A]	אדמה	soil, land, arable land, territory. Red earth. Earth of primordial humanity. Earth of Adam.
Geburah	Gaye	גיא	Valley, undulating ground like the side of a valley (Key 18).
Tiphareth	Neshiah[B]	נשיה	Oblivion, limbo. Pasture or meadow land.
Netzach	Tziah	ציא	dryness, aridity, wilderness. Sandy or desert land.
Hod	Arqa[C]	(ה)ארק	Earth, ground. Fertile soil.
Yesod	Tebhel[D]	תבל	The universe, the world. Mixed earth & water, moist earth.
Malkuth	Cheled[E]	חלד	World, duration of life, lifetime

Generally, there are Seven Earths because Yesod and Malkuth are joined like the three Supernals (Kether, Chokmah and Binah). Depending on the author, Tebhel, Cheled or both are given for the Seventh Earth.

[A] Adam (אדמ): man, humanity, person. The same letters with different pronunciations, *ah.dome* meaning, red.

150

^B This word doesn't fit the idea of Earth. *Nah.see* (נשיא) means president, chief and also a heavy cloud. *Nee.sah* (נשא) means: to be raised, lifted, high, lofty. This suggests "high ground." Finally, Nee.sah (נס) means: examine, test, experiment, to tempt and suggest "proving ground."

^C I found no entry for *Arqa or Areqa* (ארקא) in Alcalay's *The Complete Hebrew English Dictionary*. However, *ar.qah* (ארקה) means fertile soil. Maybe Areqa, as noted above.

^D The same letters spell *teh.vel* or *the.bel* meaning: perversion, abomination, incest, pollution, violation of natural order. *Tee.bale* means: to spice, flavor, season, lend variety, diversify, to variegate.

^E *Cha.lad* (חלד) to rust.

The Infernal Mansions			
Sephiroth			
Supernals	Sheol	שאול	Underworld, nether regions. The Earth's depths, pit, hades.
Chesed	Abaddon[F]	אבדון	Doom, perdition, destruction, ruin, hell, abyss
Geburah	Titahion Titahian	טיטהיון	Clinging/sludge (היון) mud/clay (טיט) The Clay of Death.
Tiphareth	Bar Schauheth[G] Shacheth	באר שחת	Well/Pit (באר) Ruin (שחת). Pit of decay or Destruction.
Netzach	Tzelmoth Tzel Moth	צלמות	Shadow of (צל) Death (מות)
Hod	Shaari Moth	שערי מות	Gates of (שערי) Death (מות)
Yesod	Gehinnom Gehennom	גיהנום	Hell, valley of (גי) Hinnom (הנום)

[F] From the root, ah.vayd (אבד) means lost, spoiled, perishable.

[G] She.chayt (שחת): to spoil, waste, ruin, destroy, to sin, to act basely, to kill. With different pronunciation, shah.chayt: pit, pitfall, grave.

^{6} ALTAR APPOINTMENTS

The PFC lecture on the altar appointments is very different than the GD. It says,

"The cross within the triangle, apex downwards placed upon the altar at the base of the Tree of Life, refers to the Four Rivers of Paradise, while the angles of the triangle refer to the Three Sephiroth Netzach, Hod and Yesod.

The two Pillars, right and left of the Tree, are the symbols of Active and Passive, Male and Female, and Adam and Eve. They allude to the Pillars of Fire and Cloud, which guided the Israelites in the wilderness. The Pillars further represent the two Kerubim of the Ark; the right Metatron, male; the left Sandalphon, female.

Above them ever burn the lamps of their Spiritual Essence, the Higher Life of which they are partakers in the Eternal Uncreated One."

[7] MAGIC SQUARE OF THE MOON

Kamea means Magic Square. This is the same magic square, using numerals instead of Hebrew letters.

Moon Magic Square								
37	78	29	70	21	62	13	54	5
6	38	79	30	71	22	63	14	46
47	7	39	80	31	72	23	55	15
16	48	8	40	81	32	64	24	56
57	17	49	9	41	73	33	65	25
26	58	18	50	1	42	74	34	66
67	27	59	10	51	2	43	75	35
36	68	19	60	11	52	3	44	76
77	28	69	20	61	12	53	4	45

[8] MAGIC LINE OF THE MOON

For more information on Magic Squares and planetary magic, see *Magic of the Planets*.

[9] SOHAM

All sources agree. Beryl in Hebrew is *tar.she.ysh* (תרשיש). It's used in Exodus 28:20 and 39:13. Pat Zalewski, in *Inner Order Teachings of the Golden Dawn* (p.109), says Soham (שהם) relates to Obsidian.

CHAPTER 3

3 = 8 RITUAL

GRADE OF PRACTICUS

Golden Dawn (GD) and the Paul Foster Case (PFC) Practicus Ritual are similar. There is minor editing of the speeches and some deletions in the PFC ritual.

If I find an image online, it's included. Otherwise, I omit them.

OPENING OUTLINE

0=0 OPENING (Short Form)

3=8 OPENING

THE SIGNS OF PRACTICUS

PURPOSE OF THE WORK

      Lesser Invoking Pentagram Ritual of Water

ADORATION

INVOCATION

DECLARATION

      END OF OPENING

ADVANCEMENT

1ˢᵀ POINT

ADMISSION

THEORICUS SIGNS AND TOKENS

OBLIGATION

THE 31ˢᵗ PATH OF FIRE – Shin (ש)

> Solar Fire
> Terrestrial Fire
> Astral Fire
> Latent Heat

EA's ADDRESS

EA's LECTURE

> Admission Badge – Pyramid of Flame
> 31ˢᵗ Path – Perpetual Intelligence
> Key 20 – Judgement

A-n and A-t's LECTURE

> Seven Heavens
> Seven Palaces
> Ten Adverse Sephiroth

MYSTIC TITLE

> Lord/Lady of the 31ˢᵗ Path

END OF 1ˢᵀ POINT

2nd POINT

30th PATH OF RESH

ADMISSION

THE 30th PATH OF THE SUN – Resh (ר)

    Summer Solstice
    Winter Solstice
    The Equinoxes
    The Sun

EA LECTURE

    Admission Badge – Solar Greek Cross
    30th Path – Collecting Intelligence
    Key 19 – The Sun

A-n and A-t's LECTURE

    Five-Fold Fire
    The Four Tides
    Planetary Symbols
    Concentric Circles Diagram
    The Tree of Alchemy

MYSTIC TITLE

    Lord/Lady of the 30th Path

END OF 2ND POINT

3rd POINT

PRACTICUS CEREMONY

ADMISSION

Badge – Octahedron

LECTURES

Garden of Eden Diagram
The Portals
Practicus Signs and Tokens
Hod – Perfect Intelligence
Baldric of Practicus
Tablet of Water
Altar Arrangement
Kamea of Mercury
Magic Line of the Mercury
Alchemical Mercury on the Tree of Life
Planets Resumed in Mercury
Functions of Consciousness on the Tree of Life
Four Planes
Seven Planes
Tarot on the Tree of Life

MYSTIC TITLE

Monoceros/Monocera de Astris and the symbol of
Mem.

PROCLAMATION

END OF ADVANCEMENT

CLOSING

ADORATION

THE PRAYER OF THE UNDINES

LICENSE TO DEPART - UNDINES

    Lesser Banishing Pentagram Ritual of Water

PRACTICUS CLOSING DECLARATION

0=0 CLOSING (Short Form)

END OF CEREMONY

Differences Between the

PFC and Golden Dawn Rituals

OPENING RITUAL

The PFC ritual opens in the Neophyte Grade by declaration of the EA, then proceeds to the 3=8 opening.

The PFC ritual adds chanting to the PURPOSE OF THE WORK.

In the DECLARATION, the GD ritual uses a battery of 9 knocks of three, each 1-3-1-3. In the PFC ritual, it's 3-2-3.

The WATER Tablet. Paul Case does not use the Enochian Tablets. Instead, Hebrew is used to derive a different tablet. Therefore the Secret Names of God and the King of the West differ.

1ST POINT

THE PATH OF FIRE ²

The SOLAR and TERRESTRIAL FIRE sections are the same in both rituals, except the PFC deletes the last paragraph.

PFC moves the last paragraph to the LATENT HEAT section in the ASTRAL FIRE section. Also, PFC deletes two-thirds of the LATENT HEAT compared to the GD ritual.

KEY 20 – JUDGEMENT. The PFC and the GD Tarot decks are different, and therefore the explanations of the keys are different.

The PFC ritual deletes the SEVEN HEAVENS, THE SEVEN PALACES and THE TEN ADVERSE SEPHIROTH sections from the Golden Dawn Ritual. These sections were added back in other esoteric orders using this ritual.

2nd POINT

THE PATH OF THE SUN

The PFC ritual omits the sections:

OLYMPIC SPIRITS.

GEOMANTIC FIGURES. This section is in the
2 = 9 ritual.

3rd POINT

CEREMONY OF PRACTICUS

ADMISSION BADGE

     GD – A Cup of Water

     PFC – a blue octahedron

REQUIREMENTS FOR OPENING & 1ST POINT

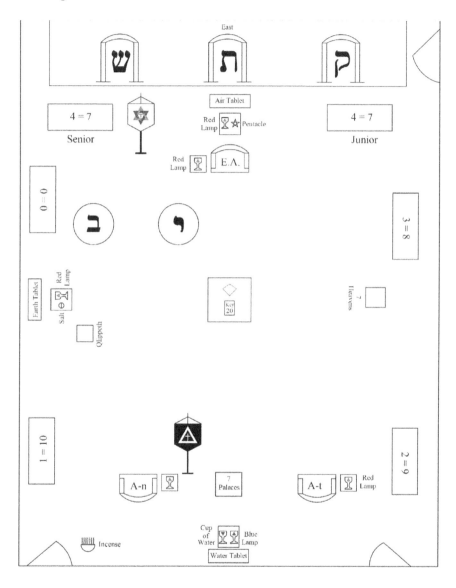

REGALIA

CHIEFS

PG with scepter, lamen, and violet mantle.

Pr-l with Scepter of Unity, lamen and blue mantle.

I-r with Scepter of Pentalpha, lamen, and red mantle.

C-s with Scepter of Reconciliation, lamen, and yellow mantle.

OFFICERS

EA with Scepter of Dominion, lamen, and red mantle.

A-n with the sword, lamen, and black mantle.

A-t with Scepter of Equilibration, lamen, and white mantle.

H-r with lamen, lamp and staff.

C-n with lamen, censer and incense.

P-r with lamen and the cup of Water

ALL

1=10 and above clothed with white robes, aprons, and baldricks.

TEMPLE SETUP

EAST

Air Tablet.

The table with a lamp is at the EA's right. Portal of Shin, Tav and Qoph as shown in the diagram below.

WEST

Water Tablet.

The station of A-n is in the northwest, facing east. A table with a red lamp is on the A-n's right.

SOUTH

The station of A-t is in the southwest, facing east. A table with a red lamp is on the A-t's right.

NORTH

Earth Tablet.

PILLARS

Placed in the Northeast, Black to North, White to South, with space between for passage of two persons.

Winged disk (see Appendix 6) with the letter Shin (ש) between the pillars.

ALTAR

Altar cloth as in Neophyte Grade. Key 20 at the center of the altar top. Solid triangular pyramid placed east of Key 20.

BANNERS

Banner of the East to the EA's right.

Banner of the West to the A-n's right.

3 = 8 Baldric

One for each candidate.

ELEMENTAL TABLETS

NORTH

Tablet of Earth, black-draped, on a music stand. A table before the tablet holds a red lamp on the east and a paten on the west.

EAST

Air Tablet, yellow-draped, on a music stand. A table before the tablet holds a red lamp on its north and a pentacle on the south.

WEST

Water Tablet, blue-draped, on a music stand. A table before the tablet holds a blue lamp on its south side and a cup of water on the north.

ADVANCEMENT REQUIREMENTS

ADMISSION BADGE

Solid Triangular Pyramid.

HOODWINK

One for each candidate.

PORTALS/PATHS

Portals of Shin, Tav and Qoph.

PEDESTALS/TABLES

One for each officer (3). Earth, Air and Water Tablets (3). One for each diagram (3). 9 total.

ADDITIONAL INSTRUCTIONS

During the opening ceremony in the Grade of Theoricus, members not holding office never leave their places. Only officers move from their stations. When there is no advancement, meetings of this grade are held in a Temple arranged for the second point because all members have attained the full grade.

Words in **bold** are chanted.

RITUAL OF 3=8

GRADE OF PRACTICUS

0=0 OPENING (Short Form)

All: *Wait outside the temple.*

EA: *Before the Opening, after the temple has been arranged, the EA closes the door and inspects the temple. When all is in order, the EA opens the door, strikes the doorpost with one rap of his/her scepter and says:*

EA: * Fellow Initiates, take your stations and places.

EA goes to the throne and remains standing, facing west.

All: *A-n enters first, followed by A-t and Practici. All go to their stations and places and remain standing. A-n and A-t face east. Practici faces north. All clothe themselves for labor.*

EA: Be seated. (*All sit.*) (Frater/Soror)_____, please perform the Lesser Banishing Ritual of the Pentagram. (*Done*)

EA: *** (*Rises. turns with the Sun to face east.*)

All: (*Rise and face east*)

EA: *(Raising scepter aloft)* Hidden Forces of that Limitless Light which establisheth the boundaries of the universe, we invoke ye by the all-powerful name of your creator (pause) to seal in just orientation the inner limits of this temple. May the secret virtue of the radiant east be conferred this day upon the throne of the Adept of this Temple, who is the emblem of that Dawning Light which shall illuminate the paths of the unknown and shall guide us to the attainment of the Quintessence, the Stone of the Wise, perfect Wisdom and true Happiness.

All: So may it be! *(All face as usual.)*

EA: Dispensing with all further ceremony, I now declare _____ Lodge, No._, open in the Grade of Neophyte!

EA: *

A-n: *

A-t * *(All remain standing.)*

3=8 OPENING

EA: * * * Fratres et Sorores of the (*name of organization*) _____, assist me to form this Temple in the Grade of Practicus. (Frater/Soror) A-t, see that the temple is properly guarded.

A-t: *Salutes with Grade sign, checks doors, returns to the station, then says:*

A-t: * Very Honored EA, the temple is properly guarded.

THE SIGNS OF PRACTICUS

EA: Honored A-n, assure yourself that none below the Grade of Practicus be present.

A-n: Fratres et Sorores give the sign of Practicus.

All: *All but A-n and EA give signs and hold the sign.*

A-n: Very Honored EA . . . *(gives the sign to EA who returns it)* . . . all present have seen the Vision of the Eternal Splendor.

All: *EA sits. All sit.*

PURPOSE OF WORK

EA: (Frater/Soror) A-t, name the element to which this Grade is attributed so that it may be awakened in the sphere of this temple and in the spheres of those who are present.

A-t: The Element of Water.

EA designates a member to perform the Lesser Invoking Pentagram Ritual of Water.

EA: Honored A-n, of what influence is this Grade the sphere?

A-n: The influence of Mercury.

(Optional: Astral Temple meditation by EA)

EA: (Frater/Soror) A-t, through what path did you approach this Grade?

A-t: Through the Thirty-first Path of Shin, ascending from Malkuth.

EA: To what does the Thirty-first Path allude?

A-t: To the manifestation of the Fire of the Spirit in the regeneration of man; to the control of the powers of the Sun and Moon in the Microcosm; to the bond of union between North and South; and to the Pyramid of Flame.

EA: Honored A-n, through what path did you complete your entrance to this Grade?

A-n: Through the Thirtieth Path of the letter Resh, ascending from Yesod.

EA: To what does the Thirtieth Path allude?

A-n: To the influence of the Sun in the release of man from the bonds of matter; to the perfection of the science of the interior stars; to the hidden forces of the south; and to the Cross of the Powers of the Zodiac.

EA: (Frater/Soror) A-t, to what path is the Grade of Practicus attributed?

A-t: To the eighth path of Hod, the Eternal Splendor.

EA: Honored A-n, what power do we build in this Grade?

A-n: With the power of the Perfect Intelligence, expressed through the Intellect of Man and energized by the Influence of Mercury.

EA: * * *

All: *All rise.*

172

MEDITATION ON RESH

All: *Prolocutor or Cantor sounds the tone D. The five intonations following are all on this pitch.*

EA: **THOUGH I AM THE GREATEST OF THE GREAT,** (*hold*)

A-n: **I AM ALSO THE SMALLEST OF THE SMALL.** (*hold*)

A-t: **I AM THE DEPTH AS WELL AS THE HEIGHT,** (*hold*)

EA: **THE WITHOUT AS WELL AS THE WITHIN.** (*hold*)

All: *(Including members, intone)*:
FOR IN ME ARE ALL OPPOSITES UNITED.

EA: Let us adore the Lord and King of Water.

All: *All face west.*

ADORATION

EA: *Make a clockwise circle with THE scepter toward the west.*

ELOHIM TZABAOTH, Creative Power of Hosts, be Thy Name perfected in the minds of all. Glory be unto the Ruach Elohim, who moved upon the face of the Waters of Creation.

All: **AMEN**. (*All give the sign of the Grade.*)

INVOCATION

A-n: *Unveils the Earth Tablet.*

EA: *Unveils Air tablet in the east, then moves west,
passing the altar on its Northern side. Unveils
the Water Tablet. All others remain at stations
and places, facing west. With his/her scepter,
he/she makes the following figures before the
Tablet of Water:*

EA: And the Elohim said: "Let us make Adam in our
image, after our likeness, and let them have
dominion over the fish of the sea."

In the name EL, strong and powerful, and in the
name of **ELOHIM TZABAOTH**, Spirits of Water,
adore your creator!

*(Takes Cup from the pedestal. Make the sign for
Scorpio* ♏ *in the air before the tablet.)*

In the name **GABRIEL**, great Archangel of Water,
and in the sign of the Death which leads to
Regeneration, Spirits of Water, adore your
creator!

In the names of the Great Western Quadrangle[1]...

(makes + with Cup before the Tablet) . . .

Spirits of Water, adore your creator!

(Elevates Cup and holding it on high says): In the three great Secret Names of God, borne on the Banner of the West:
V_'_E, G_ _ _ _ _'_ _A, R_ _ _ _ _'_ _O, Spirits of water adore your creator!

In the name M_ _ _'MI R_ _ _'_ _ _ _A, great King of the Sea, Spirits of Water, adore your creator!

Replaces Cup. Returns to the throne and takes the scepter.

All: *All face as usual and remain standing.*

DECLARATION

EA: In the name **ELOHIM TZABAOTH**, I declare this temple to be formed as a mirror of the Universal Substance by the power of the Perfect Intelligence, energized by the Fire of Spirit and the radiance of the Eternal Sun.

EA: * * *   * *   * * *

A-n: * * *   * *   * * *

A-t: * * *   * *   * * *

EA: *Sits.*

All: *All sit.*   END OF OPENING

ADVANCEMENT

1st POINT

Temple is arranged for the Ritual of the 31st Path, as in the diagram. The temple lights are dimmed.

EA: Fratres et Sorores, our (Frater/Soror) ____, having made such progress in the path of Occult Science as has enabled him/her to pass through an examination in the requisite knowledge, is now eligible for advancement to the Grade of Practicus, and I have received dispensation to advance (him/her) in due form.

(Frater/Soror) A-t, superintend the preparation of the Theoricus and give the customary alarm.

ADMISSION BADGE

Pyramid of Flame

A-t: *Rises, salutes with Grade sign, goes to the altar and takes hoodwink and admission badge. Leaves Temple, closing portal behind him/her. Theoricus is robed and wearing the apron and baldric of Theoricus. A-t gives him/her the Pyramid of Flame, to be held in his/her right hand, and says:*

A-t: This is the Pyramid of Flame. It is your admission badge to the Path of the Perpetual Intelligence.

Theoricus is then hoodwinked and led to the portal.

A-t knocks with the battery of the Grade:

* * *   * *   * * *

A-n: *Opens the door, admits them, and returns to their seat after closing the door behind them.*

A-t: *Halts just inside the door and says:*

His throne was like a fiery flame, and the wheels as burning fire.

Conducts Theoricus to the west and turns him/her so he/she faces the A-n. A-t takes the Pyramid of Flame from the Theoricus.

SECRET SIGNS AND TOKENS

A-n: *(Rises)* Give me the sign of the Grade of Theoricus (Done).

Give me the grip. *(Done)*

Give me the Grand Word. *(Shaddai el Chai)*

The Mystic Number? *(45)*

The password?
Theoricus says Mem,
A-n says Heh,
Theoricus says, Mah.

A-n: Give me also the Mystic Title and Symbol you received. *(Poraios de Rejectis. Ruach.)*

A-t: *Turns candidate, facing him/her east.*

A-n: *Sits.*

OBLIGATION

EA: (Poraios/Poraia) de Rejectis, do you solemnly pledge to maintain the same strict secrecy concerning the mysteries of this Grade of Practicus that you have already promised to maintain, respecting those of the preceding Grades?

A-t: *Prompts Theoricus to answer if necessary and then places him/her so that he/she faces the tablet of Water.*

EA: Then you will stretch forth your hand, in the position of the Saluting Sign of Neophyte, and say: "I swear by the abyss of the Waters." *(Done)*

Let the hoodwink be removed.

A-t: *Removes hoodwink from Theoricus. Takes Cup of Water from the pedestal before the Tablet and places it in the left hand of the Theoricus.*

EA: Sprinkle with your right hand a few drops of water toward the Tablet in the west, and say:

"Let the powers of Water witness my pledge." *(Done)*

A-t: *Takes Cup from Theoricus and replaces it on the pedestal.*

EA: Conduct the Theoricus to the Northeast and place him/her before the Mystic Pillars.

A-t: *Conducts Theoricus to just West of the Pillars as commanded.*

RITUAL OF THE 31st PATH

EA: You now stand symbolically in the Grade of Zelator, facing the portal of the Thirty-first Path, which leads from the Grade of Zelator to that of Practicus.

Take in your right hand the Pyramid of Flame, and follow your guide, which leads you through the Path of Fire.

THE PATH OF FIRE

A-t: *Leads Theoricus through the pillars, passes EA and goes round the temple with the Sun, halting before the EA after one complete circumambulation.*

SOLAR FIRE

EA: *Rises as they approach, holding Red Lamp in his/her hand, and says:*

I am the apex of the Pyramid of Flame. I am the Solar Fire, pouring forth its beams on the lower world, life-giving, light-producing.

By what symbol dost thou seek to pass by?

A-t: By the symbol of the Pyramid of Flame.

EA: Hear thou the words of our wise brethren of ancient days:

"The Mind of the Father whirled forth in a re-echoing roar, comprehending by invincible Will ideas omniform, which, flying forth, from that One Fountain issued.

For from the Father alike were the Will and the End, whereby they are connected with the Father, according to alternating life, through varying vehicles.

The Foundation of All is One and Alone. From this, the others rush forth and are distributed and separated through the various bodies of the universe, being borne in swarms through its vast abysses, ever whirling forth in illimitable radiation.

They are intellectual conceptions from the Paternal Fountain, partaking abundantly of the brilliance of Fire in the culmination of unresting time.

The primary self-perfect Fountain of the Father pours forth these primogenial ideas. These being many, ascend flashingly into the Shining Worlds, containing the Three Supernals.

Thus did the Creator of All, self-operating, form the world, first bringing forth a certain mass of Fire, producing all these varying vehicles so that the cosmic body might be completely conformed.

From Fire did all proceed. To Fire do all return. Therefore, in Fire, all things live and move. For that which is One and Alone is Eternal Spiritual Fire." *(Sits.)*

A-t: *Leads Theoricus to the seat of the A-n, where they halt facing him/her.*

181

TERRESTRIAL FIRE

A-n: *Rises, holding lamp as they approach. After they halt, facing A-n, he/she says:*

I am the left basal angle of the Pyramid of Flame. I am the Fire, volcanic and Terrestrial, flashingly flaming through the abysses of Earth. Fire rending, Fire penetrating, Fire tearing aside the curtain of matter, Fire constrained and tormented, raging and whirling in a lurid storm.

By what symbol dost thou seek to pass by?

A-t: By the symbol of the Pyramid of Flame.

A-t leaves Theoricus before A-n and returns to his/her station.

A-n: Hear ye the words of the wise:

Not in matter did the Fire which is beyond the First enclose his power in acts, but in Mind; for the fashioner of the fiery world is the Mind of Mind, who first sprang from Mind, clothing the one Fire with the other Fire, and binding them together so that He might mingle the Fountainous craters while preserving, unsullied, the brilliance of His own Fire.

"From whence proceedeth a fiery whirlwind, drawing down the brilliance of the flashing flame, penetrating the abysses of the universe. From thence, downwards, all extend their wonderous rays, abundantly animating Light, Fire, Aether, and the Universe."

Replaces lamp on the pedestal, steps forward, and leads Theoricus, by way of the Sun, around the temple, past EA, to the seat of A-t.

182

ASTRAL FIRE

A-t: *Rises as they approach, holding Red Lamp. When they halt before A-t, he/she says:*

I am at the right basal angle of the Pyramid of Flame. I am Fire, Astral and Fluid, winding and coruscating through the firmament. I am the life of beings, the vital heat of existence.

By what symbol does thou seek to pass by?

A-n: By the symbol of the Pyramid of Flame.

A-t: Hear the words of the wise again:

"The Father hath withdrawn himself but hath not shut up his own Fire in his intellectual power. All things are sprung from that One Fire, for all things did the Father of all perfect, and delivered them to the Second Mind, whom all races of men call First." *(Sits)*

A-n: *Conducts Theoricus to the East of the Altar, around the Temple with the Sun. When East of Altar, A-n turns Theoricus so that he/she faces east. Then, A-n returns to his/her station and sits.*

LATENT HEAT

EA: *(Seated, says):* The Soul, being a brilliant fire, by the power of the Father, remaineth immortal, and is the mistress of life, and filleth up the many recesses of the bosom of the world, the channels being intermixed, wherein she performeth the works of incorruptible Fire.

Such a Fire existeth, extending through the rushings of Air. There is also a Fire formless, whence cometh the Image of a Voice - a flashing light, abounding, whirling forth, crying aloud.

Stoop not down unto the darkly splendid world, wherein continually lieth a faithless depth, and Hades wrapped in clouds, delighting in unintelligible images, precipitous, winding, a black, ever-rolling abyss; ever espousing a body unluminous, formless and void.

Stoop not down, for a precipice lieth beneath the earth, reached by a descending ladder which hath seven steps, and established the throne of an evil and fatal force.

Explore, however, the river of the soul, whence, and in what order you have come; so that, although you have become a servant to the body, you may rise again to the Order from which you descended, joining works to sacred reason.

A-t: *Leaves station, goes to Theoricus, and conducts Theoricus by way of the Sun through the pillars to the throne of the EA. The A-t takes the Pyramid of Flame from the Theoricus and hands it to the EA when facing the EA.*

A-n: *Turns up lights as A-t and Theoricus pass through the pillars.*

LECTURES

ADMISSION BADGE

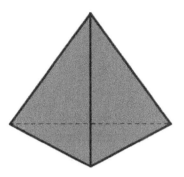

EA: The solid, triangular pyramid, or tetrahedron, is an appropriate fire glyph. It comprises four triangles, three visible and one concealed, yet it synthesizes the rest. The three visible triangles represent fire: Solar, volcanic or Terrestrial; and Astral, while the fourth represents the Latent Heat.

PERPETUAL INTELLIGENCE

EA: The Thirty-first Path of Wisdom, corresponding to the letter Shin (ש), is called the Perpetual Intelligence. Herein is the secret fire which regulates the motion of the Sun and Moon in their proper order. Your work as Practicus concerns the direction of this secret fire.

   Rises and leads Theoricus to the altar. Theoricus is placed west, facing alter. EA stands on the north side during the lecture on Key 20.

A-t: *A-t follows and stands on the south side of the altar.*

EA: Before you on the altar is the Twentieth Key of the Tarot, which symbolizes the inner meaning of the thirty-first Path. To the uninitiated eye, it represents the Last Judgement, with an angel blowing a trumpet and the dead rising from their coffins. Still, its meaning is far more occult and recondite than this, for it is a glyph of the Powers of Fire.

The angel represents Gabriel, the great archangel, ruler of the Element of Water, to which this Grade is attributed. Yet, is this Water truly Fire, and thus do alchemists agree that they use the Secret Fire hidden in the Element of Water to practice their art.

The trumpet represents the influence of the Spirit, descending from Binah, while the banner with the cross refers to the four rivers of Paradise and to the letters of the Holy Tetragrammaton.

The right-hand figure below is Samael, ruler of Volcanic or Terrestrial Fire. He corresponds to Osiris, and his posture refers to that god of the ancient Egyptians.

The left-hand figure is Haniel, the ruler of Astral Light. She corresponds to Venus, Ceres, Persephone, and the Egyptian Isis.

With his back turned, the central lower figure is Arel, the angel of Fire and ruler of Latent Heat, corresponding to the Egyptian Horus.

EA: *Returns to their throne and sits.*

MYSTIC TITLE

EA: * * * (Rises)

All: *All rise.*

EA: I have much pleasure in conferring on you the title of (Lord/Lady) of the Thirty-first Path. You will now quit the temple for a short time, and on your return, the ceremony of your passage through the Thirtieth Path will take place. (*Sits*)

All: *Sit.*

A-t: *Leads Theoricus with the Sun to the antechamber.*

END OF 1st POINT

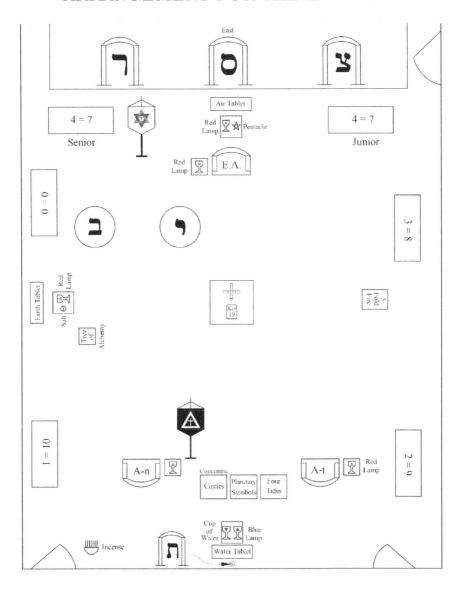

CHANGES FOR 2ND POINT

EAST

As in the diagram, portals are changed to Resh, Samekh, and Tzaddi.

WEST

Portal of Tav above the Tablet of Water. Shown to the side of the drawing for clarity.

SOUTH

Diagram of 5-Fold Fire.

NORTH

Tablet of Earth. Tree of Alchemy diagram.

ALTAR

Key 19 in place of Key 20.

ADMISSION BADGE

The solar Greek Cross of 13 Squares is placed on the altar while setting up the temple for the Ritual of the 30th Path. Placed east of Key 19.

PILLARS

Between the Pillars is the letter Resh (ר) held to the winged disk[1] with Velcro.

RITUAL OF THE 30th PATH

Temple is arranged as in the diagram for the 30th Path. Lights dimmed. All seated.

EA: (*Seated at the throne, says*): (Frater/Soror) A-t, you have my command to present the Theoricus with the necessary admission badge and admit him.

A-t: *Rises and gives the sign of Grade to EA. Goes to the altar, picks up the admission badge, and goes to the antechamber.*

ADMISSION

A-t: *Gives Theoricus the Greek Cross to hold in his/her right hand, says:*

This is the Solar Greek Cross. It is your admission badge to the Path of the Collective Intelligence.

Then leads Theoricus into the temple. As they enter, the A-t says:

Behold, He hath placed His tabernacle in the Sun.

Leads Theoricus to the Northeast, facing pillars, and remains at his/her side.

EA: Frater/Soror (Poraios/Poraia) de Rejectis, three portals lead from the Grade of Theoricus to the Grade beyond. Of these, the only one now open to you is the Thirtieth, which leads to the Grade of Practicus. Hold in your right hand the Solar Greek Cross, and follow your guide through the Pathway of the Sun.

PATHWAY OF THE SUN

A-t: *Leads Theoricus between pillars and the foot of the EA's throne. They halt, facing EA.*

SUMMER SOLSTICE

EA: *Rises, hold Red Lamp, and says:*

I am the Sun in greatest elevation, bringing upon earth the ripening heat, fructifying all things, urging forward the growth of vegetable nature; life-giving, light-producing, crowning summer with golden harvest, and filling the lap of plenteous autumn with the purple vintage of the vine. (*Sits*)

A-t: *Leads Theoricus to the seat of the A-n.*

WINTER SOLSTICE

A-n: *Rises, holding Red Lamp, and says:*

I am the Sun in greatest depression beneath the equator when cold is greatest, and heat is least, withdrawing his light in darkening winter, the dweller in mist and storm. (*Sits.*)

A-t: *Leads Theoricus to A-t's own seat.*

THE EQUINOXES

A-t: *Picks up Red Lamp and turns to face Theoricus, saying:*

I am the Sun in Equinox, initiating summer or heralding winter, mild and genial in operation, giving forth or withdrawing the vital heat of life.

Replaces lamp on the pedestal, leads Theoricus West of the altar and faces Theoricus toward East.

THE SUN

EA: The Father of all congregated the seven firmaments of the cosmos, circumscribing the heaven with convex form. He constituted a septenary of wandering existences - suspending their disorder in well-disposed zones. He made them six in number, and for the seventh, He cast into the midst thereof the Fiery Sun, that center of resounding light from which all lines are equal.

A-t: *Conducts Theoricus with Sun, to EA, passing between the pillars. Halts facing EA, takes the cross from Theoricus and hands it to EA Remains beside Theoricus.*

A-n: *Turns lights back up as the A-t and Theoricus pass between the pillars. Returns to the station and sits.*

ADMISSION BADGE

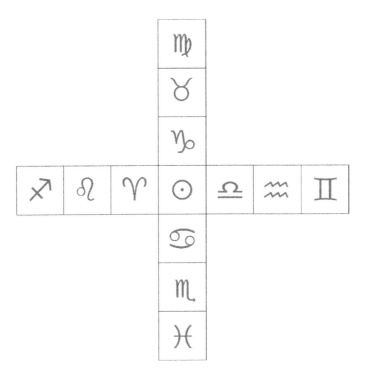

EA: The Solar Greek Cross is formed of thirteen squares which fitly refer to the Sun's motion through the Zodiac, these signs being arranged in the arms of the cross according to the four elements, with the Sun in the center, thus representing that luminary as the center of the whole.

COLLECTIVE INTELLIGENCE

EA: The Thirtieth Path of Wisdom, corresponding to the letter Resh, is called the Collective Intelligence. This path links the Grade of Theoricus to that of Practicus. A text giving a more detailed explanation of its meaning and the meaning of the Thirtieth Path will be available for your studies in this Grade.

EA/A-t:

EA rises. Goes to the altar, followed by A-t and Theoricus. EA at the north side of the altar, Theoricus West of the altar, and A-t at the south side.

EA: Before you on the altar is the nineteenth Key of Tarot, which symbolizes the meaning of the Thirtieth path of Wisdom.

The face of the Sun symbolizes the truth that the day star is a great center of life and consciousness, akin to the life and consciousness of man.

Its 8 principal rays are alternately waved and salient, symbolizing the alternation of the masculine and feminine natures.

Besides these are forty-eight other rays, arranged in groups of three, to show the threefold activity of solar power as fashioning, maintaining and transforming all things.

Thus the total number of rays is 64, the square of the number 8, to which the Grade of Practicus is specially referred.

The thirteen Hebrew Yods falling from the Sun refer by their number to unity and love because 13 is the value of the Hebrew nouns corresponding to these words.

The wall is of stone, laid in five courses, to represent the five senses. It symbolizes those limitations that your training in occult science practice will enable you to overcome. Yet it is of stone, an ancient symbol for truth and union, because your work, even though it may enable you to transcend the limits of physical sensation, will not require you to deny such truths as may be discovered by the right use of physical sense.

The sunflowers represent five stages in the manifestation of life in physical form. They are sunflowers to show that solar radiation makes all such manifestations here on Earth possible. Four of them, fully open, represent respectively the mineral, vegetable, animal and human kingdoms. The fifth, yet in the bud, symbolizes the Fifth Kingdom, composed of beings who have advanced beyond the limitations of natural humanity.

Dancing in a fairy ring, the two children are types of regenerated humanity. At the stage represented by this key, the regeneration is yet at its beginning.

A tradition of our Order also says that the boy represents the element of earth, the girl the element of water, while the Sun and the letters Yod refer to the elements of fire and air.

(EA returns to the throne and sits.)

A-t: *Leads the candidate to the south.*

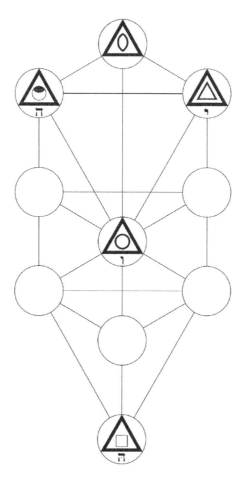

A-t: Frater/Soror (Poraios/Poraia) de Rejectis, the Ancients noted the numeral correspondence of the phrase "Ruach Elohim." Spirit of God, with the letter Shin, the emblem of Fire. The fire was to them a fitting symbol of Spirit, for Fire is the transforming element, breaking down forms outworn so that they may be remolded into a more perfect expression of the Life-Power.

The diagram before you represents the different forms of Fire assigned to the Sephiroth.

Spirit or Akasha of Fire is assigned to Kether. Chokmah, the "Root of Fire," corresponds to Fire of Fire.

Binah, "Root of Water," is assigned Water of Fire. Air of Fire is assigned to Tiphareth. Finally, Terrestrial Fire corresponds to Malkuth.

Thus, the One Fire of Spirt manifests in different modes, from the Throne of Thrones to the Garden of Eden.

A-t takes the candidate to the southwest.

THE FOUR TIDES

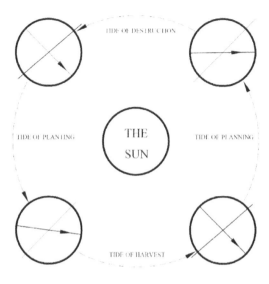

VERNAL EQUINOX   WINTER SOLSTICE

TIDE OF DESTRUCTION

TIDE OF PLANTING   THE SUN   TIDE OF PLANNING

TIDE OF HARVEST

SUMMER SOLSTICE   AUTUMNAL EQUINOX

A-t: *Face the diagram of the Four Tides.*

A-t: My Brother (Sister), there are tides in the
Unseen, and the success of our magical working
depends very largely upon the set of those tides.
They are of several kinds and produce different
results. We may roughly divide them into five
types:

Stellar, Solar, Planetary, Lunar and Terrestrial.
In actual work, the influences of the stellar,
solar and lunar tides work upon us through the
magnetic sphere of the Earth since they produce
their effect in the sphere of the Earth. We,
Children of Earth and the race of the Starry
Heavens, respond to the varying tides of our
mother planet.

As the Earth rotates on its axis and travels simultaneously around the Sun, stress centers are set up in the magnetic sphere of the Earth. Any part of the earth's surface sends a positive current from East to West during the daytime. So there is a steady current or tide in the magnetic sphere of the earth, flowing from East to West. When we align our temples to the east, it is in recognition of this flow.

As the Earth moves around the Sun, a magnetic current passes from the north to the south for six months, and the reverse is the case for the remaining six months. These "seasonal" tides are also of great practical value. They are marked by the solstices and equinoxes and are classified as follows:

The Tide of Planning: From the Autumnal Equinox to the Winter Solstice.

The Tide of Destruction: From the Winter Solstice to the Spring Equinox.

The Tide of Planting: From the Vernal Equinox to the Summer Solstice.

The Tide of Harvest: From the Summer Solstice to the Autumnal Equinox.

Of course, these Tides are not so sharply defined; they merge one into the other and the "cusps," where this merging takes place, are of mixed influence. Ecclesiastes's author says, "There is a time for sowing and a time for reaping, a time to be born and a time to die, and for everything under the sun, there is a time."

A-t: *Returns to station.*

202

PLANETARY SYMBOLS

○ = ALCHEMICAL SUN & GOLD   ☽ = ALCHEMICAL SILVER & MOON   ✝ = DEATH & CORROSION

⊙ = ○

☽ = ☽

♂ = ☿

♀ = ○

♃ = ♃

☿ = ♃ = ♄

A-n: A-n approaches and conducts the candidate to the west by the Planetary Symbols diagram.

A-n: Frater/Soror (Poraios/Poraia) de Rejectis, the astrological symbols of the planets are derived from the 3 primary forms: the circle, crescent and the cross, either singly or in combination. The circle denotes the Sun and gold, the crescent the Moon and silver, respectively, analogous to the Red and the White alchemical natures. The cross is the symbol of corrosion. The color of corrosion is usually complementary to its natural color. Thus, copper, which is reddish, becomes green in verdigris etc.

Mercury is the only one of the planetary symbols which unite these primary forms in one symbol. Saturn is composed of the Cross and the Crescent, showing that lead is corrosive externally and Lunar internally. Jupiter is the reverse. Mars is solar internally, while Venus is the opposite, for copper is external to the nature of gold but internally corrosive. Therefore, the Sphere of Venus Nogah's name denotes External Splendor.

DIAGRAM OF CONCENTRIC CIRCLES

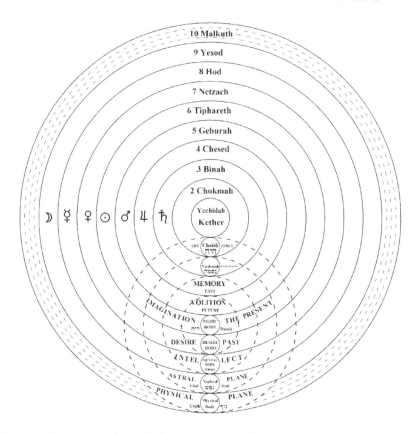

A-n: *Escorts Candidate to Northwest, to the diagram of the Concentric Circles.*

A-n: The Tree of Life is not the only manner representing the Ten Sephiroth. This diagram, showing them as concentric circles, is given in many older Qabalistic writings.

The central circle is Kether, and the successive concentric circles are attributed to the remaining Sephiroth.

The main purpose of this diagram is to indicate the principles of the human constitution in a manner less confusing than the Tree of Life diagram. It shows plainly that Yekhidah in Kether is humanity's central, innermost principle. From the center of this Kether, a circle runs a radius of the whole system of circles, corresponding to the thread-soul of human personality. The small circles whose Hebrew names and English text clearly show what they represent.

The center of the personal system is the EGO in Tiphareth. Thus, the personality constitution is represented by the concentric dotted circles surrounding the small circle representing the Egoic body. Note that no circles represent bodies or vehicles in the larger circles of Chesed and Geburah, corresponding to memory and volition. These are cosmic powers that are not embodied.

There are, therefore, seven vehicles, indicated by this diagram:

1. The Causal Body, corresponding to Chaiah, the Life-force;
2. The Buddhic body, a vehicle of the Divine Soul;
3. The Egoic Body, a vehicle of Ruach;
4. The Desire body;
5. The Mental Body;
6. The Astral Body;
7. The Physical Body.

Some occult systems also speak of an etheric body, but the Qabalistic schools hold that this is one of the subtler aspects of the physical body and do not count it as a separate vehicle.

(*Archon returns to his/her station.*)

TITLE

LORD/LADY OF THE 30th Path

A-t: *A-t conducts Theoricus to the West of the Altar, facing the east, returns to his/her station and remains standing.*

EA: * * * (*Rises*)

All: *All rise.*

EA: I have much pleasure in conferring upon you the title of Lord/Lady of the 30th Path. You will now quit the temple for a short time, and on your return, the ceremony of your entry into the Temple of Hod will take place.

EA: *Sits.*

All: *Sit.*

A-t: *Leads Theoricus with the Sun to the antechamber.*

END OF 2ND POINT

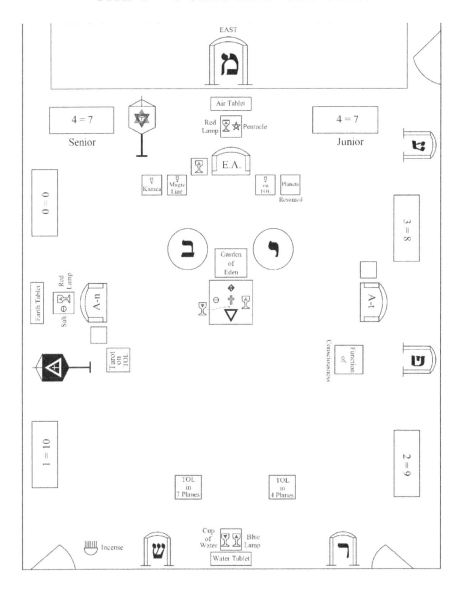

TEMPLE SETUP

EAST

Portal of Mem, above Air Tablet. Near the EA are diagrams: Kamea of Mercury, Magical Line of Mercury, Alchemical Mercury on the Tree of Life, and Planetary Symbols Resumed in Mercury.

SOUTH

Portal of Ayin in the Southeast. Peh in the South. Portal of Resh in the Southwest. A-t seated in the station is usually occupied by the C-n.

WEST

Portal of Shin in the northwest.

NORTH

Station of A-n. Tablet of Earth.

ALTAR

Diagram of the Garden of Eden east of the altar with orange cloth. The admission badge is the octahedron. Altar is arranged as in Neophyte Grade, except a white triangle is pointing west, a cup of water east of the triangle, and a red cross placed east of the cup (the cup joins the triangle with the cross).

PILLARS

Pillars are slightly east of the altar, as in the diagram.

PEDESTALS/TABLES

One for each officer (3). One for each tablet (3). Six for the diagrams (illustrations by EA can have two per tablet). 12 total.

3rd POINT

THE GRADE OF PRACTICUS

Temple is arranged as in the diagram, brightly lighted and members seated.

EA: (Frater/Soror) A-t, instruct the Theoricus in the proper alarm, present (him/her) with the necessary admission badge, and admit (him/her).

A-t: *Gives sign of the Grade; takes octahedron, goes to Theoricus and says:*

This is the Octahedron. It is your admission badge to the Temple of Hod.

Brings the Theoricus, instructing him/her to knock.

*** ** ***

ADMISSION

A-t/Theo: * * *   * *   * * * *(They enter.)*

EA: By what symbol dost thou enter herein?

A-t: By the special emblem of this Grade, the octahedron.

EA: Advance to the East.

THE ADMISSION BADGE

OCTAHEDRON

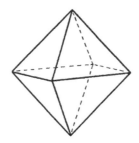

A-t: *Conducts Theoricus with Sun to the foot of the throne of the east. Takes octahedron from Theoricus, gives it to the EA, and remains standing with the Theoricus.*

EA: The octahedron is this Grade's special emblem because it is a regular solid having eight equal faces. Thus it corresponds particularly to the power of the number 8.

This solid, moreover, is closely related to the cube, for both cube and octahedron have exactly thirteen axes of symmetry. But, again, a cube has six faces, twelve boundaries, and eight corners, so the sum of the numbers required to describe its proportions is 26. Similarly, the octahedron has eight faces, six corners and twelve boundaries. Therefore, the sum of the numbers required to set forth its proportions is also 26, the special number of the Tetragrammaton.

When placed as I hold it now, the face of the octahedron turned toward you shows the down-pointing triangle of the element of Water, to which this Grade is referred, and the base of the solid is also, relatively to you, a water triangle.
The other three sides, now visible to you, form fire

triangles. Two support the water triangle facing you; the third is the top of the octahedron. This is a symbolic representation of the union of the powers of water and fire in alchemical Mercury, also referred to in this Grade of Practicus.

If the solid is reversed so that the top, as you observe it, becomes a water triangle, the two triangles on either side will be water triangles also, and the face immediately before you will be a fire triangle.

Our ancient brethren, observing these and other peculiarities of the octahedron, saw in it a fitting emblem of the fiery fluid alchemists most commonly designated as "their water" or "their Mercury."

This fiery fluid is symbolized by the Sun's rays in the nineteenth Key of the Tarot. The children in that picture represent the same thing, sometimes called "Rebis," in reference to its duality in various forms of manifestation.

A more extended explanation of the symbolic meaning of the octahedron is given in a special lecture belonging to this Grade.

EA rises and goes to the altar, instructing the Theoricus and the A-t to follow. EA stands north of the altar, west of the black pillar, facing the altar.

A-t: *Leads Theoricus, follows EA to the altar, and places Theoricus west, facing east. A-t stands south of the altar, west of the white pillar, facing the altar.*

EA: The diagram before you represents the symbolism of the Garden of Eden. At the summit is the Supernal Eden, containing the three Supernal Sephiroth, summed up and contained in Aima Elohim, the Mother Supernal, the woman of the twelfth chapter of the Apocalypse, clothed with the Sun, and with the Moon under her feet. On her head is a crown, symbolic of Kether, surmounted by 12 stars.

And, whereas the name Tetragrammaton is joined to the name Elohim when it is said that "Tetragrammaton Elohim planted a garden eastward in Eden," this represents the power of the Father joined to it in the glory from the face of the Ancient of Days.

In the Garden were the Tree of Life and the Tree of the Knowledge of Good and Evil. This latter tree is from Malkuth, the lowest Sephirah, between the rest of the Sephiroth and the Kingdom of Shell. That kingdom is represented by the Great Red Dragon coiled beneath, having seven heads (the Seven Infernal Palaces) and ten horns (The Ten Averse Sephiroth of evil contained in the seven palaces.)

And the river Nahar went forth out of Eden (namely from the Supernal Triad), to water the Garden (the rest of the Sephiroth), and from thence it was divided into four heads in Da'ath, whence it is said: "In Da'ath the depths are broken up, and the clouds drop down dew."

The first head is Pison, which flows into Geburah, whence there is gold. It is the River of Fire. The second is Gihon, the River of Waters, flowing into Chesed. The third is Hiddekel, the River of Air, flowing into Tiphareth. And the fourth, which receives the virtues of the other three, is Phrath, or the Euphrates, which flows down upon Malkuth, the Earth.

The river going out of Eden is the River of the Apocalypse, the Waters of Life, clear as crystal, proceeding out of the throne of God and the Lamb, on either side of which was the Tree of Life, bearing twelve manner of fruit.

Thus do the rivers of Eden form a cross, and on that cross, the great Adam, the Son who is to rule the nations with a rod of iron, is extended from Tiphareth, and his arms stretch out to Chesed and Geburah.

In Malkuth is Eve, mother of all and completion of all, and above the universe, she supports the eternal pillars of the Sephiroth with her hands.

THE PORTALS

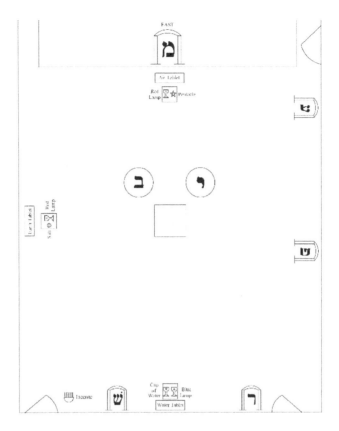

EA: The Grade of Practicus is referred to as the Sephirah Hod, which is approached by the 31st (ש) and 30th (ר) Paths. Therefore, the portals of these paths are behind you in the southwest. From this Grade, there are three paths on the Way of Return. They are the paths of the letters Peh (פ), Ayin (ע) and Mem (מ), whose portals are shown in the south, southeast, and east. Not yet may you pass these portals, though all lead from this Grade of Practicus.

SIGNS AND TOKENS

EA: The title of this Grade refers to the active practice of magical works based on the theoretical principles in which you have already received instruction. Certain documents from this Grade will teach you the elements of these practical procedures.

The Grade sign is given thus: with the hands together, raise the arms till the elbows are level with the shoulders. Then, with the thumbs and forefingers, make a triangle on your breast, apex downward. (*Demonstrates it.*)

This represents the element of water to which this Grade is attributed.

The grip or token is the general grip of the First Order. The Grand Word is a name of ten letters, Elohim Tzabaoth, which means "God of Hosts." The mystical number is 36, the sum of the numbers from 1 to 8, and from it is formed the password of this Grade, which is Eloah (אלה), one of the divine Names. It is to be lettered separately when given - Aleph, Lamed, Heh - the one who gives the word pronouncing the first letter; the one who receives it the second letter; and the one who gives it pronouncing the third letter along with the password.

PERFECT INTELLIGENCE

EA: To this Grade and Sephirah Hod, the eighth Path of Wisdom is attributed to the Perfect Intelligence. It is so-called because it is the dwelling-place of the Primordial and has no root in which it may abide other than the recesses of Gedulah, whence its essence emanates.

BALDRIC OF PRACTICUS

EA: The distinguishing badge of this Grade, which you will now be entitled to wear, is the baldric of a Practicus. In the center is a cross with the numbers 3 and 8 to the left and right. Above is the letter Shin and below is Resh. They are symbolic of the 31st and 30th Paths, respectively. Below the letter Resh in Hebrew is Mem, meaning Water. Flanking each side of the numbers 3 and 8 is the symbol for Mercury.

TABLET OF WATER

ה	מ	ש	נ	ב	ר	ע	מ	נ	ו	ה	י
צ	ד	ה	ר	י	מ	ל	ה	ב	צ	ו	ג
נ	ר	מ	ר	נ	ו	ה	ת	י	ב	מ	ל
י	א	ש	פ	ל	א	ע	כ	נ	ר	כ	א
נ	ע	י	ב	ר	ק	ע	נ	ב	ד	ש	י
ד	כ	ל	ד	י	ש	ר	ט	ו	ע	ו	צ
ו	א	פ	ג	ס	מ	ת	ר	א	ר	א	י
ה	ל	כ	י	ט	י	מ	ס	ר	ל	ר	נ
ר	ס	י	מ	ל	י	ה	ד	נ	י	ת	מ
א	ה	ל	ז	ב	ו	ל	נ	ד	ב	מ	א
ו	ק	ס	א	י	צ	י	ל	ו	כ	ל	ל
ר	נ	ב	נ	ת	ד	ו	ר	י	ג	א	א
ו	נ	מ	ו	ר	י	א	ל	ב	ר	כ	י

EA: The Grade of Practicus is specially referred to as the element of Water, and therefore the Great Tablet of the West forms one of its principal emblems.

EA/A-t/Theoricus: *Turn toward the west, facing the tablet, during the EA's following description of the Tablet.*

EA: From it are drawn the three holy secret names of God: V_'_E, G_ _ _ _ _' _A, R_ _ _ _ _' _O; and numberless divine and angelic names which appertain unto the Element of Water.

ALTAR ARRANGEMENT

EA/A-t/Theo:

> *Turn to face the altar again. EA points to Cross and Triangle and says:*

EA: The cross above the triangle represents the power of the Spirit of Life, rising above the triangle of the waters and reflecting the triune. The cup of water at the junction of the cross and the triangle represents the maternal letter, Mem.

> *EA leaves the altar and goes with the Sun to the diagram of the Kamea of Mercury in the Northeast.*

A-t: *Follows EA, leading the Theoricus to the diagram of the Kamea.*

נב	סא	ד	יג	כ	כט	לו	מה
יד	ג	סב	נא	מז	לה	ל	יט
נג	ס	ה	יב	כא	כה	לז	מד
יא	ו	נט	נד	מג	לח	כז	כב
נה	נח	ז	י	כג	כו	לט	מב
ט	ח	נז	נו	מא	מ	כה	כד
נ	סג	ב	טו	יח	לא	לד	מז
יו	א	סד	מט	מח	לג	לב	יז

EA: This diagram is Mercury's Kamea or Magic Square. It comprises 64 squares, or cells, arranged eight by eight. The Hebrew letters within the cells represent the numbers one through sixty-four. The constant summation of the lines, vertical, horizontal, or diagonal, is 260, while the total number represented by the 64 cells is 2080, which is the theosophical extension of 64.

EA conducts Theoricus and A-t to the following diagram, the Magic Line of Mercury.

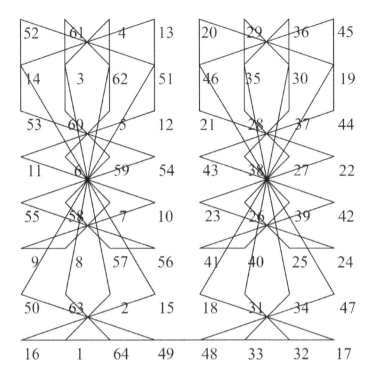

EA: This diagram is the Magic Line of Mercury, formed by drawing straight lines from center to center of the sixty-four squares in the consecutive order of their numbers. Even this casual inspection will show you how striking a symbol of equilibrium is this magic line.

From a text belonging to this Grade, you will learn further details of the occult meaning of the Kamea and its Magic Line.

EA conducts the Theoricus and A-t to the Diagram of Mercury on the Tree of Life.

ALCHEMICAL MERCURY ON THE
TREE OF LIFE

EA: This diagram shows the Alchemical symbol of Mercury on the Tree of Life. It embraces all but Kether. The horns spring from Da'ath, which is not properly a sephirah, but rather the conjunction of Chokmah and Binah.

(Conducts the Theoricus and A-t to the diagram Planets Resumed in Mercury.)

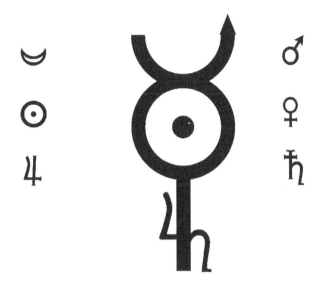

EA: Before you, here is a diagram representing the combination of the symbols of the planets to form the symbol of Mercury, the planet attributed to this Grade. In this apparently arbitrary and fanciful figure, an occult truth is concealed, which is more fully explained in a text belonging to this Grade.

Returns to the throne and sits.

A-t: *A-t comes forward, conducts the Theoricus to the west of the altar, and remains standing with the Theoricus.*

FUNCTIONS OF CONSCIOUSNESS
ON THE TREE OF LIFE

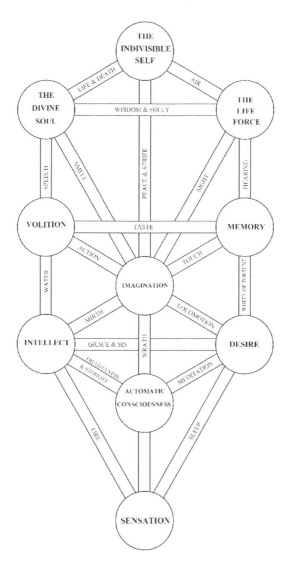

A-t: Frater/Soror (Poraios/Poraia) de Rejectis, our
ancient brethren inform us that the twenty-two
letters of flame are the foundation of all things;
for He who formed the universe has formed,

weighed, and composed these twenty-two letters into every created thing; and the form of everything which shall hereafter be.

Three mothers, seven doubles, and twelve simples, all but parts of one living body. One above three, three above seven, and seven above twelve, all connected one with the other.

Before you is a symbolic representation of the unity of 3, 7 and 12, operating as Functions of Consciousness in the Universal Mind and the Mind of Man.

Three Fathers, Air, Water, and Fire spring from the Three Mothers.

From the Seven Doubles come forth the Seven Opposites, for the seven are called double because each letter presents a contrast, or permutation, of its inherent quality of goodness. Thus we have life and its opposite of Death; Wisdom and its opposite of Folly; Peace and Strife; Wealth and Poverty; Grace and Sin; Fruitfulness and Sterility, and Dominion and Slavery.

The twelve simple letters are the foundations for the twelve qualities of sensory perception: Sight, Hearing; Smell; Speech; Taste; Touch; Work; Locomotion; Wrath; Mirth; Meditation, and Sleep.

Conducts Theoricus to the four Planes of Consciousness diagram in the southwest of the Tree of Life.

FOUR PLANES

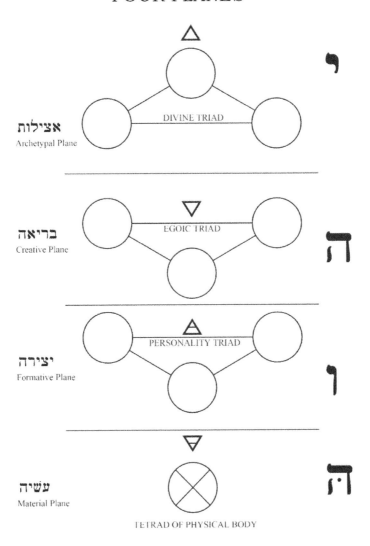

אצילות
Archetypal Plane

DIVINE TRIAD

 בריאה
Creative Plane

EGOIC TRIAD

יצירה
Formative Plane

PERSONALITY TRIAD

עשיה
Material Plane

TETRAD OF PHYSICAL BODY

A-t: Frater/Soror (Poraios/Poraia) de Rejectis, in the Grade of Theoricus, you learned of the soul, the Occult Constitution of Man, and its subdivision into many parts.

Before you is a diagram of the soul or the occult constitution of Man on the Tree of Life, subdivided

228

into Four Planes of Consciousness and answering the Four Qabalistic Worlds.

The highest plane, corresponding to Atziluth, is the Divine Triad and includes the Sephiroth Kether, Chokmah and Binah.

The next plane is the Egoic Triad, corresponding to Briah, and includes the Sephiroth Chesed, Geburah and Tiphareth.

Below the Egoic Triad is the Personality Triad, corresponding to Yetzirah, consisting of the Sephiroth Netzach, Hod and Yesod.

Lastly is the Tetrad of the physical body, consisting of Malkuth and the four elements corresponding to the Qabalistic world of Assiah.

A-n: *Archon comes forward and conducts the Theoricus to the following diagram, the Seven Planes.*

A-t.   *Returns to their station and sit.*

SEVEN PLANES

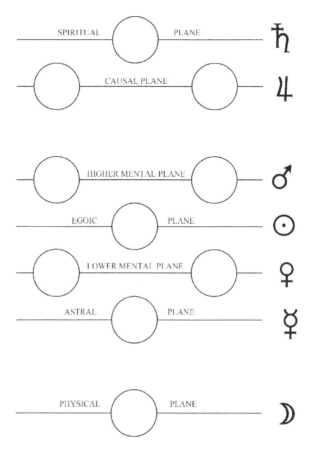

A-n: Frater/soror (Poraios/Poraia) de Rejectis, in the teachings of our ancient brethren, mention is often made of Seven Celestial Spheres or Planes, which lead from the Material to the Spiritual, and answer by analogy to the seven planets of the ancients in a manner different than you have previously learned.

Also, in the recent teachings of some of our brethren, mention is made of seven planes of consciousness leading to the union with the

Divine Self, the Indivisible Self Qabalists term the Yechidah.

Before you is a diagram of the Tree of Life, arranged into Seven Planes, answering to the Seven Planets of the ancients and the Seven Planes of Consciousness.

Thus, Saturn answers to Kether and the Spiritual Plane; Jupiter answers to Chokmah and Binah and the Causal Plane; Mars answers to the Higher Mental Plane and to the Sephiroth Chesed and Geburah; the Sun answers to Tiphareth and the Egoic Plane; Venus answers to Netzach and Hod, and the Lower Mental Plane; Mercury answers to Yesod, and the Astral Plane; while Luna corresponds to Malkuth and the Physical Plane.

Conducts Theoricus to the diagram of the Tarot on the Tree of Life in the North.

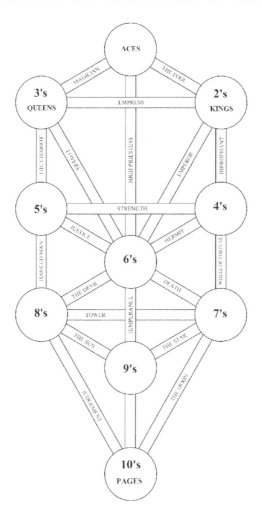

A-n: Frater/Soror (Poraios/Poraia) de Rejectis, before you, is a diagram that shows the true and genuine attribution of the Tarot Keys to the Tree of Life.

The four Aces correspond to the Throne of Kether, with the remaining small cards of each suit corresponding to the numbered Sephirah: twos

(2s) to Chokmah, threes (3s) to Binah, and so on.

The twenty-two trumps, or Major Arcana, are assigned to the letters of the paths between the Sephiroth.

While the court cards, answering to the four letters of the Holy Tetragrammaton, are assigned to their respective Sephiroth: The Kings to Chokmah; the Queens to Binah; the Knights or Princes to Tiphareth; and the Knaves, Princesses, or Pages to Malkuth.

A-t: *The architect comes forward and conducts the Theoricus to the west of the altar and remains standing with the Theoricus.*

A-n.   *Returns to the station and sits.*

MYSTIC TITLE

EA: (*Sitting, says*): I now congratulate you on having attained the Grade of Practicus, and in recognition thereof, I confer upon you the mystic title of (Monoceros/Monocera) de Astris, which means "Unicorn from the Stars," and I give you the symbol of Mem, which is the Hebrew name for Water.

PROCLAMATION

EA: * * * (All rise)

In the name of **ELOHIM TZABAOTH**, I now proclaim that you have been duly advanced to the Grade of Practicus and that you are Lord/Lady of the Thirtieth and Thirty-first Paths.

A-t: *Conducts the new Practicus to their seat in the temple.*

All: Sit.

END OF ATTUNEMENT

CLOSING

EA: * Fratres et Sorores of the (*name of organization*) _____, assist me in closing this Temple in the Grade of Practicus.

EA: * * *

All: *Rise.*

EA: (Frater/Soror) A-t, see that the temple is properly guarded.

A-t: *Gives Grade sign, performs his/her duty, returns to their station, and says:*

  * Very Honored EA, the temple is properly guarded.

EA: Let us adore the Lord and King of Water

All: All face west.

ADORATION

EA: Let **ELOHIM TZABAOTH** be praised unto the countless ages of time.

All: **AMEN**. (*All give the sign of the Grade.*)

PRAYER OF THE UNDINES

EA: *EA goes west, facing the tablet of Water.*

A-t: *A-t conducts the new Practicus to the west and places him/her behind the E.A. A-t takes up position behind and South of the EA.*

A-n: *The A-n comes forward with the rest of the officers and takes up position behind and to the north of the EA.*

All: *Members, in their places, are still facing west.*

(Water Tablet in the West)
EA

A-t   Pract   A-n

H-r

C-n   P-r

EA: Let us rehearse the Prayer of the Undines:

> Terrible King of the Sea, thou who holdest the keys of the cataracts of heaven, and who enclosest the subterranean waters in the cavernous hollows of the earth - King of the deluge and of the rains of spring, Thou who openest the sources of the rivers, and of the fountains; Thou who commandest moisture, which is as the blood of the earth, to become the sap of plants - we adore Thee, and we invoke Thee.

236

Speak thou unto us, thy mobile and changeful creatures, in the great tempests, and we shall tremble before Thee. Speak to us in the murmur of limpid waters, and we shall desire thy love.

O Vastness, wherein all the rivers of being seek to renew themselves, which renew themselves ever in Thee!

O Thou Ocean of Infinite Perfections!
O Height which reflectest Thyself in the Depth!
O Depth which exalts into the Height!

Lead us into true life, through intelligence, through love!

Lead us into immortality through sacrifice, that we may be found worthy to offer one day unto Thee, the blood and the tears, for the remission of sins.

All: **AMEN.**

EA: *With a scepter, makes the following figures in the air before the Tablet of Water:*

EA: Depart ye in peace unto your habitations. May the blessing of **ELOHIM TZABAOTH** be upon you. Be there peace between you and us, and be ye ready to come when ye are called.

EA: * EA veils Water Tablet, then Air Tablet.*

A-n: Return to stations. A-n veils the Earth tablet.

All: *Practicus goes to his/her seat, and all face as usual.*

EA: *Sits. All sit.*

EA: Frater/Soror _____, please perform the Lesser Banishing Pentagram of WATER.

The designated member performs the Banishing Ritual.

PRACTICUS CLOSING DECLARATION

EA: I now declare this temple closed in the Grade of Practicus.

    * * *   * *   * * *

A-n: * * *   * *   * * *

A-t: * * *   * *   * * *

0=0 CLOSING (Short Form)

EA: *If the meetings of other Grades do not follow the 3=8 Closing, then the EA proceeds to close the temple in the Grade of Neophyte, saying:*

Dispensing with all further ceremony, I now declare this temple closed as a Hall of Neophytes of the *(name of organization)*_____.

EA: *

A-n: *

A-t: *

END OF CEREMONY

239

CHAPTER 3 NOTES

[1] TRACING THE EQUAL-ARMED CROSS

The cross is drawn with the lines traced on top of each other. The lines are shown below with separation to emphasize the directions – start in the center, trace top to bottom, back to center, then right to the left.

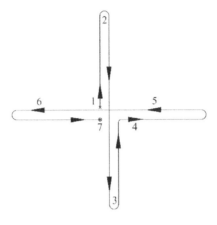

^{2} SEVEN HEAVENS,

10 ADVERSE SEPHIROTH,

7 PALACES

These sections were deleted in the Paul Case ritual. However, the information in The Golden Dawn is valuable, so I am including it here.

SEVEN HEAVENS

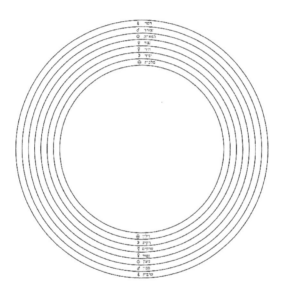

Frater/Soror (Porais/Poraia) de Rejectis, our ancient brethren, further informed us that the Seven Double letters, He who created all things, designed, produced, combined and formed with them: Seven Planets; Seven Worlds; Seven Heavens; Seven Earths; Seven Rivers; and Seven Seas.

Before you is a symbolic representation of the Seven Heavens in Assiah, the Material World.

The 1st is *Ghereboth*, referred to as Chesed, wherein are the Treasures of Blessings.

The 2nd is *Mekon*, referred to as Geburah, wherein are the Treasures of the Spirit of Life.

The 3rd is *Maghon*, referred to as Tiphareth, wherein are Angels.

The 4th is *Zebel*, referred to as Netzach, wherein is the Supernal Altar, whereon Michael the great High Priest sacrifices the Souls of the Just.

The 5th is *Shachaqim*, referred to as Hod, wherein is the manna.

The 6th is *Raquie*, wherein are the Sun and Moon, the Stars and Planets and all the 10 Spheres; it is called Yesod.

The 7th Heaven is *Velun,* referred to as Malkuth, wherein is the *Shamayim*, or Heavens containing 18,000 worlds. And *Thebel*, the World between Eden and *Gehennah*.

End of Golden Dawn text

The Seven Heavens have listed Godwin's Cabalistic Encyclopedia, p. 138.

	Traditional	Hebrew	Sephiroth
7	Araboth	ערבות	Supernals
6	Makhon	מכון	Chesed
5	Maon	מעון	Geburah
4	Zebul	זבול	Tiphareth
3	Shehaqim	שחקים	Netzach
2	Rakia	רקיע	Hod
1	Vilon	וילון	Yesod & Malkuth

The Golden Dawn gives the name of the 7th (or 1st) Heaven Arabhoth. The GD ritual has the first letter Ayin (ע), an "A" sound. Therefore I believe this is a spelling error in English.

Araboth traditions mean "plains," but Alcalay's Hebrew English Dictionary as heaven. The same letters are pronounced *a.ray.vut* means pleasantness, sweetness.

Makhon: site, place, dwelling, city, established place, foundation.

Maon: habitation, house, refuge, residence, den, lair.

Zebul: high, celestial palace.

Shehaqim: heavenly, celestial. *Sha.chaq* (שחק): clouds, heaven.

Rakia: expanse, canopy, the vault of heaven, firmament, heavens, sky.

Vilon: veil, curtain, hanging drape, velum.

Note Golden Dawn attributes *Araboth* to Chesed, while Godwin says Supernals.

243

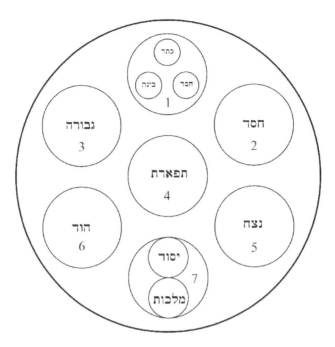

Frater/Soror (Porais/Poraia) de Rejectis, our brethren of old penetrated deep into the mysteries of the Number Seven, for it is said that He, who created all things, preferred the number Seven above all things under His Heaven.

Before you is a diagram representing the Ten Sephiroth united into Seven Palaces, the understanding of which affords the key to many mysteries of the number seven.

The first palace contains Kether, Chokmah, and Binah; the second palace contains Chesed; the third palace contains Geburah; the fourth, Tiphareth; the fifth, Netzach; the sixth, Hod; and the seventh, Yesod and Malkuth.

TEN ADVERSE SEPHIROTH

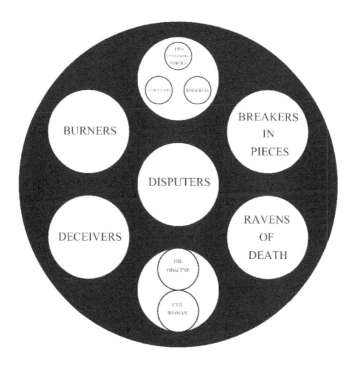

Frater/Soror (Porais/Poraia) de Rejectis, contiguous to
the material universe, resides the Qlippoth: a place of
chaos and confusion wherein the shells of the dead
and evil exist forces inimical to humanity.

Before you are the 10 Averse and Evil Sephiroth of the
Qlippoth or Shells, collected into 7 Palaces wherein is
the Apocalyptic mystery of the 7 heads and 10 horns.

The Qlippoth of Kether are the two contending Forces.

The Shells of Chokmah are the Hinderers.

Those of Binah are the Concealers.

Those of Chesed are the Breakers in pieces.

To Geburah belong the Burners.

To Tiphareth the Disputers.

To Netzach, the Ravens of Death, dispersing all things.

To Hod the deceivers.

To Yesod the Obscene.

And the Shell of Malkuth is Lilith, the Evil woman. These Evil Sephiroth also have many other names.

CHAPTER 4

4 = 7 RITUAL

GRADE OF PRACTICUS

Golden Dawn and the Paul Foster Case (PFC) Practicus Ritual are similar. However, Paul Case deletes large sections from the Golden Dawn Ritual.

Like the three previous rituals, the opening and closing are very similar. However, the Paul Case ritual has deleted or altered many guardians' speeches. Also, some of the diagrams and instructions are deleted.

If I find the image online, it's included. Otherwise, I omit them.

4 = 7 RITUAL

GRADE OF PHILOSOPHUS

OPENING

0=0 OPENING (Short Form)

4=7 OPENING

THE SIGNS OF PHILOSOPHUS

PURPOSE OF THE WORK

> Lesser Invoking Pentagram Ritual of FIRE

ADORATION

INVOCATION

DECLARATION

END OF OPENING

1ST POINT

29th PATH OF QOPH

ADMISSION

PRACTICUS SIGNS AND TOKENS

OBLIGATION

THE 29th PATH OF WATER – Qoph (ק)

    Stagnant Waters
    Turbid Waters
    Pure Waters
    Gathering Waters

EA's LECTURE

    Admission Badge – Cross of 12 Squares
    29th Path – Corporal Intelligence
    Key 18 – The Moon

TITLE

    Lord/Lady of the 31st Path

END OF 1ST POINT

2ND POINT

28th PATH OF TZADDI

ADMISSION

THE 28th PATH OF TZADDI – (צ)

> Rain
> Dew
> Mists and Clouds
> The Three Supernals

EA'S LECTURE

> Admission Badge – Cube of Balanced Forces
> 28th Path – Natural Intelligence
> Key 17 – The Star

MYSTIC TITLE

> Lord/Lady of the 28th Path

END OF 2ND POINT

3RD POINT

27th PATH OF PEH

ADMISSION

    Badge – Cross of 10 Squares

ADMISSION

THE 27th PATH OF PEH – (פ)

    Kings of Edom

EA'S LECTURE

    Admission Badge – Cross of 10 Squares
    30th Path – Exciting Intelligence
    Key 16 – The Tower

TITLE

    Lord/Lady of the 27th Path

PROCLAMATION

END OF 3rd POINT

4TH POINT

Ceremony of Philosophus

ADMISSION

Badge – Calvary Cross of 6 Squares

EA'S LECTURE

The Fall Diagram
Signs and Tokens of Philosophus
Occult or Hidden Intelligence
Baldric of Philosophus
Fire Tablet
Altar Appointments

Kamea (Magic Square)
Magic Line of Venus
Venus on the Tree of Life
Trinity on the Tree of Life

MYSTIC TITLE

Pharos Illuminans and the symbol of Esh.
The further title is "Honored," and the symbol is
Phrath.

PROCLAMATION

A-n's ADDRESS

END OF 4th POINT AND ATTUNEMENT

CLOSING

ADORATION

THE PRAYER OF THE SALAMANDERS

LICENSE TO DEPART - Salamanders

    Lesser Banishing Pentagram Ritual of FIRE

PRACTICUS CLOSING DECLARATION

0=0 CLOSING (Short Form)

END OF CEREMONY

DIFFERENCES BETWEEN THE RITUALS

OPENING

The PFC ritual opens in the Neophyte Grade by declaration of the EA. Then the ceremony proceeds to open in the grade of Philosophus.

The GD ritual uses a battery of knocks, 3-3-1.
PFC uses 3-1-3.

1ST POINT [2]

1. FIRE Tablet. Paul Case does not use the Enochian Earth Tablet. Instead, Hebrew is used to derive an entirely different tablet. Therefore the Secret Names and King of the South are different.

2. The EA's lectures are similar in the two rituals. The PFC rituals delete texts from the GATHERING WATERS section.

3. The PFC ritual deleted these sections: THE SERPENT OF BRASS, QABBALA OF THE 9 CHAMBERS [see end of chapter notes], HEXAGRAM OF TIPHARETH, GEOMANTIC FIGURES OF 8 RADII (Case moved the geomantic figures to the 2 = 9 ritual).

2ND POINT ³

1. The GD Admission Badge is a four-sided pyramid. The PFC badge is the green Cube of Balanced Forces. Therefore the explanatory lecture is different, and the Key 17 – The Star.

2. PFC has completely rewritten THE THREE SUPERNALS section.

3. These sections are deleted in the PFC ritual: SPELLING OF IHVH IN THE 4 WORLDS [see end of chapter notes], DIAGRAM OF THE DEKAGRAM, ENDEKAGRAM, DODEKAGRAM (Case moved the lineal figures to the 2 = 9 ritual)... and CUPUT AND CAUDA DRACONIS.

3RD POINT ⁴

1. The PFC ritual deletes a few paragraphs of the KINGS OF EDOM section.

2. The PFC and GD Tarot decks are different. Therefore the descriptions KEY 16, The Towers, are different.

3. The PFC rituals delete these sections in the GD ritual: ALCHEMICAL SYMBOL OF SULPHUR ON THE TREE OF LIFE [see the end of chapter notes], TABLET OF 7 YETZIRATIC PALACES IN 10 SEPHIROTH, TABLET OF QLIPPOTH WITH 12 PRINCES.

4TH POINT [5]

1. The PFC ritual deletes paragraphs of the GD ritual in THE FALL section.

2. FIRE TABLET. GD uses Enochian Tablets. PFC made his own tablets derived from Hebrew.

3. The PFC rituals delete these sections in the GD ritual: TREE OF LIFE WITH DAATH, TREE OF LIFE IN FOUR WORLDS [see end of chapter notes], BURNT OFFERING, and BRAZEN SEA.

CLOSING DIFFERENCES

The Secret Names and King of the North differ in the two rituals because of the different FIRE tablets. The PRAYER TO THE SALAMANDERS section was edited but essentially the same.

4 = 7 PHILOSOPHUS

REQUIREMENTS FOR OPENING & 1ST POINT

REGALIA

CHEIFS

PG with scepter, lamen, and violet mantle.

Pr-l with Scepter of Unity, lamen and blue mantle.

I-r with Scepter of Pentalpha, lamen, and red mantle.

C-s with Scepter of Reconciliation, lamen, and yellow mantle.

OFFICERS

At the right hand of each officer is a pedestal with a Cup of Water.

EA in the Northeast, facing west, with Scepter of Dominion, lamen and red mantle.

A-n in the West, facing east, with sword, lamen and black mantle.

A-t in the Southeast, facing west, with Scepter of Equilibration, lamen and white mantle.

H-r with lamen, lamp and staff.

C-n with lamen, censer and incense.

P-r with lamen and the cup of Water

GRADE MEMBERS

Clothed with a white robe, apron, and baldricks.

The two most senior 4=7 to the south of the Air station, facing west (behind EA) and the next two most senior 4=7 similarly to the north of the Air station. The remaining 4=7 sit around the perimeter of the temple.

TEMPLE SETUP

EAST

Above and behind the station of Air Tablet is the Portals of Shin, Tav and Qoph.

SOUTH

Fire Tablet.

WEST

Water Tablet.

NORTH

Earth Tablet.

PILLARS

The pillars are in the southeast, facing east, black to the north, and white to the south.

The Winged disk (see Appendix 6) with the letter Qoph (ק) is between the pillars.

ALTAR

Placed at the center of the temple with the Elemental Altar Cloth. Cross of 12 Squares east of Key 18.

BANNERS

Banner of east to the right of EA.

Banner of West to the north of A-n.

ELEMENTAL TABLETS

NORTH

Tablet of Earth, black-draped, on a music stand. A table before the tablet holds a red lamp on the east and a paten on the west.

EAST

Air Tablet, yellow-draped, on a music stand. A table before the tablet holds a red lamp on its north and a pentacle on the south.

WEST

Water Tablet, blue-draped, on a music stand. A table before the tablet holds a blue lamp on its south side and a cup of water on the north.

SOUTH

Fire Tablet, red-draped, on a music stand. A table before the tablet holds a red lamp on its east side and a censer and incense on the west.

LARGE PORTALS

Shin, Tav, Qoph, Resh, Samekh, Tzaddi, Mem, Ayin, Peh, Kaph, Nun.

SMALL PORTALS FOR WINGED DISK

Qoph, Tzaddi, Peh

KEYS FOR ALTAR

Key 16, 17, 18

ADMISSION BADGES

1st Point: Cross of 12 Squares
2nd Point: Green Cube of Balanced Forces
3rd Point: Cross of 10 Squares
4th Point: Red Calvary Cross

DIAGRAMS

Diagram of the Fall
Kamea of Venus
Magic Line of Venus
Venus on the Tree of Life
Trinity on the Tree of Life

LAMPS

7 red, 2 blue

PEDESTALS/TABLES

One for each officer (3). One for each elemental tablet (4).

ADVANCEMENT REQUIREMENTS

The admission badge is the Cross of Twelve Squares.

Hoodwink

4 Cups

Elemental and Green Altar cloths

Pentacle

Small Qoph, Tzaddi, and Peh portals.

Incense for Venus

4=7 Baldrick

RITUAL NOTES

During the Opening ceremony in the Grade of Philosophus, members not holding office never leave their places. Only the officers move from their stations. When there is no advancement, meetings of this grade are held in a Temple arranged as for the Fourth Point because all members have attained the full grade.

Words in **bold** are chanted.

RITUAL OF 4=7

GRADE OF PHILOSOPHUS

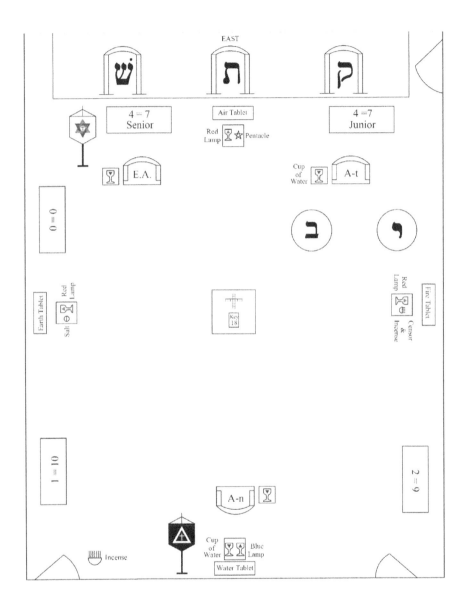

0=0 OPENING (Short Form)

All: *Wait outside the temple.*

EA: *Before the Opening, after the temple has been arranged, the EA closes the door and inspects the temple. When all is in order, the EA opens the door, strikes the doorpost with one rap of his/her scepter and says:*

EA: * Fellow Initiates, take your stations and places.

        EA goes to throne, remains standing facing west.

All.   *A-n enters first, followed by A-t and Philosophi. After that, all go to their stations and places and remain standing.*

EA: Be seated. *(All sit.)* Honored
        (Frater/Soror) _____, please perform the
        Lesser Banishing Pentagram Ritual of
        Earth. *(Done)*

EA: *** *(Rises, turns with the Sun to face east.)*

All.   *Rise and face east.*

EA: *(Raising scepter aloft)* Hidden Forces of that Limitless Light which establisheth the boundaries of the Universe, we invoke ye by the all-powerful name of your creator *(pause)* to seal in just orientation the inner limits of this temple. May the secret virtue of the radiant east be conferred this day upon the throne of the Adept of this Temple, who is the emblem of that Dawning Light which shall illuminate the paths of the unknown and shall guide us to the attainment of the Quintessence, the Stone of the Wise, perfect Wisdom and true Happiness.

263

All.   So may it be! *(All face as usual.)*

EA: Dispensing with all further ceremony, I now declare _____ Lodge, No.__, open in the Grade of Neophyte!

EA: *

A-n: *

A-t: *   *All remain standing.*

4=7 OPENING

EA: * * *   Fratres et Sorores of the (*name of organization*) _____, assist me to form this Temple in the Grade of Philosophus. (Frater/Soror) A-t, see that the temple is properly guarded.

A-t: Salutes with Grade sign, checks doors, returns to the station, then:

     *   Very Honored EA, the temple is properly guarded.

THE SIGNS

EA: Honored A-n, assure yourself that none below the Grade of Philosophus be present.

A-n: Fratres et Sorores, give the sign of Philosophus.

All: *All but EA: and A-n give the sign, holding it through A-n's following speech, then:*

A-n: Very Honored, EA...

     (*A-n gives the sign, followed by EA*)

     ....all present have partaken of the Divine Victory.

EA: *Sits.*

All: *Sit.*

PURPOSE OF THE WORK

EA: (Frater/Soror) A-t, name the element to which this grade is attributed so that it may be awakened in the spheres of those present and in the sphere of this temple.

A-t: The element of Fire.

EA: Honored (Frater/Soror)____, perform the Lesser Invoking Pentagram Ritual of Fire. (*Done.*)

EA: Honored A-n, of what influence is this grade the sphere?

A-n: The influence of Venus.

(*Optional: Guided meditation by EA*)

EA: (Frater/Soror) A-t, through what path did you first approach this grade?

A-t: Through the Twenty-ninth Path of the letter Qoph, ascending from Malkuth.

EA: To what does the Twenty-ninth Path allude?

A-t: To the manifestation of the Water of Formation in the embodiment of man; to the Secret Path of Return; to the reflection of the Sphere of Pisces; and to the Cross of the Zodiac.

EA: Honored A-n, through what path did you continue your approach to this grade?

A-n: Through the Twenty-eighth path of the letter Tzaddi, ascending from Yesod.

EA: To what does the Twenty-eighth path allude?

A-n: To the manifestation of the Life-breath in the renewal of man's mind; to the revelation of truth; to the balanced disposition of the interior stars; to the reflection of the Sphere of Aquarius; and to the Cube of Balanced Forces.

EA: (Frater/Soror) A-t, through what Path did you complete your entrance to this grade?

A-t: Through the Twenty-seventh Path of the letter Peh, proceeding from Hod.

EA: To what does the Twenty-seventh Path allude?

A-t: To the influence of Mars in releasing the human mind from the bonds of delusion; to the secret of creative intelligence; to the hidden forces of the north; and to the Cross of the Sephiroth.

EA: Honored A-n, to what Path is the Grade of Philosophus attributed?

A-n: To the Seventh Path of Netzach, the Divine Victory.

EA: (Frater/Soror) A-t, what power do we build in this grade?

A-t: With the power of the Occult Intelligence, expressed through the desire of humanity and energized by the influence of Venus.

EA: * * *

All: *Rise. Prolocutor or Cantor sounds the tone F-sharp. The following intonations are all on this pitch.*

EA: I AM VICTORIOUS

A-n: BEFORE EVER THE BATTLE IS JOINED,

A-t: AND THE CONTINUANCE OF MY LIFE

All: IS AN EFFULGENT SPLENDOR THROUGHOUT ETERNITY.

ADORATION

EA: Let us adore the Lord and King of Fire.

All: *Face South.*

EA: *Makes with scepter a clockwise circle toward the south.*

       YOD HEH VAV HEH TZABAOTH, Ruler of the Hosts of Heaven, be Thy Name Victorious in the Hearts of all. Praised be the Daughter of the Voice, speaking from the midst of the Hidden Fire.

All: **AMEN**. (*All give the sign of the grade.*)

A-n: *Moving with the Sun, unveils Earth Tablet and returns to the station.*

A-t: *Moving with the Sun, unveils Water tablet and returns to the station.*

EA: *Unveils Air Tablet, then goes to the south, passing the altar on its eastern side.*

All: *Remain at stations and places facing south.*

INVOCATION

EA: *Unveils Fire Tablet. With a scepter, makes the following figures before the Tablet of Fire:*

And the Elohim said: Let us make Adam in our image, after our likeness, and let them have Dominion.

In the Name, **ELOHIM**, living and victorious; in the Name, **YOD HEH VAV HEH TZABAOTH**, Spirits of Fire, adore your creator!

Takes censer from the pedestal; makes the sign of Leo ♌ *in the air before the Tablet:*

In the name, **MICHAEL**, great Archangel of Fire, and in the sign of the secret power in all spiritual activities, Spirits of Fire, adore your creator! In the names and letters of the Great Southern Quadrangle[1]...

(*makes* ✝ *with censer before Tablet*)

...Spirits of Fire, adore your creator!

(*Holding censer on high*) In the three great Secret Names of God, borne on the banner of the South: **HEHELA VALASHISHI REASHILA**, Spirits of Fire, adore your creator!

Makes a large circle clockwise, with a censer, beginning at the upper point, from where he/she has been holding the censer.

In the Name, **LALAHERE - REASHISHI**, Great King of the South, Spirits of Fire, adore your Creator! (*Replaces censer. Returns to their station.*)

All: *Face as usual and remain standing.*

DECLARATION

EA: In the Name, **YOD HEH VAV HEH TZABAOTH**, I declare this temple to be formed as a vehicle of the Creative Fire by the power of the Occult Intelligence, operative through the influence of Venus, for the perfection of our minds and bodies in the confection of the Sacred Stone.

EA: *** * ***

A-n: *** * ***

A-t: *** * ***

EA: *Sits.*

All: *Sit.*

END OF 4=7 OPENING

1ST POINT

EA: Fratres et Sorores, our (Frater/Soror)____, (motto), having made such progress in the Path of Occult Science as has enabled (him/her) to pass an examination in the requisite knowledge, is now eligible for attunement to the Grade of Philosophus, and I have received a dispensation to advance (him/her) in due form.

(Frater/Soror) A-t, superintend the preparation of the Practicus and give the customary alarm.

ADMISSION

A-t: *Rises. Salutes with Grade sign. Takes Cross of Zodiac from the altar and leaves the temple, closing the portal behind him/her. The Practicus robed and wearing an apron, and the sash of 3=8 grade is in meditation. A-t places the Cross in Practicus's right hand, saying:*

This is the Cross of the Zodiac. It is your admission badge into the Path of Pisces, the Corporeal Intelligence.

Places hoodwink on Practicus and lead him/her to the portal. A-t knocks with the battery of the grade: *** * ***

A-n: *Opens the door, admits them and returns to their seat after closing the door behind them.*

A-t: And the Ruach Elohim moved upon the face of the Abyss of Waters.

Conducts Practicus to the west and turns him/her to face A-n. Takes Cross from Practicus.

A-n: (*Rises.*)   Give me the sign of the Grade of Practicus. (*Done*)
Give me the grip. (*Done*)
Give me the Grand Word. (*Elohim Tzabaoth*)
The Mystic Number? (36)
The password? (*Aleph, Lamed, Heh, Eloah.*)
Give me also the Mystic Title and Symbol you received. (*Monoceros de Astris. Mem.*)

OBLIGATION

A-t: *Takes Practicus to the south, facing east.*

EA: Monoceros de Astris, do you solemnly pledge to maintain the same strict secrecy concerning the mysteries of this Grade of Philosophus that you have already promised to maintain, respecting those of the preceding Grades?

Prac. I do.

EA: Then you will stretch forth your hand in the position of the Saluting Sign of Neophyte and say: "I swear by the Torrent of Fire."

Prac. I swear by the Torrent of Fire.

EA: Let the hoodwink be removed.

A-t: *Removes hoodwink, turns Practicus so that he/she faces the Tablet of Fire and gives him the censer, first making sure it is smoking.*

EA: Cense thrice toward the Tablet of Fire in the South and say: "Let the powers of Fire witness by my pledge."

Prac: (does so)

A-t: *Replaces censer on the pedestal.*

29th PATH OF QOPH

EA: Conduct the Practicus to the southeast and place (him/her) between the pillars.

A-t: *Does so. During the following speech, points out the portals named by the EA.*

EA: You now stand symbolically in the Grade of Zelator, facing the Thirty-first, Thirty-second and Twenty-ninth paths portals. The two former you have already passed, and the portal of the Twenty-ninth Path, leading to the Grade of Philosophus, is now open to you. Take the Cross of the Zodiac in your right hand and follow your guide through the Path of the Waters.

A-t: *Gives Cross to Practicus. They pass through the pillars and then circumambulate the temple 1 1/2 times, beginning at the southeast and going with the course of the Sun. As they approach the northeast for the second time, the EA rises, and they halt, facing him/her.*

STAGNANT WATERS

EA: *(Rises as they approach, holding cup)*

I am Water, stagnant, silent and still, reflecting all, concealing all. I am the Future, veiled by the reflections of what hath been. "He who shall rise from the Abyss of Waters" is my name. Hail unto ye, Dwellers in the Land of Night! Behold, the rending of darkness is at hand. *(Sits.)*

A-t: *Leads Practicus around to A-n and halt before him/her.*

TURBID WATERS

A-n: (*Rises as they approach, holding Cup.*)
I am Water, turbid and troubled. I am the Torrent of that-which-hath-been, and there is none so strong that he may resist the onward sweep of that hidden current. To the ignorant, I am the Banisher of Peace and "Storm veiled in Terror" is my name, but the wise know me as the "Giver of Limitless Substance," measuring forth to every creature the satisfaction of every need. I am the Past, shrouded in the veil of human forgetfulness. Hail unto the mighty powers of nature and the Lord of the Whirling Storm! (*Sits*)

PURE WATERS

A-t: *Leads Practicus around to his/her own station, picks up Cup and says:*

I am Water, pure and limpid after its purification by the storm, ever-flowing on toward the sea. I am the ever-passing Present, standing in the place of the Past and moving onward to unveil the Future. "The Traveller through the Gates of the Hidden Places" is my name. Hail unto ye, Dwellers in Eternity, shadowed under the wings of Dawn!

Replaces Cup. Leads Practicus to the West of the Altar, facing him/her to the East. Returns to the station and sits.

GATHERING WATERS

EA: (*Rises*) I arise in the place of the Gathering of the Waters through the rolled-back Cloud of Night. Silent and vast lay the measureless expanse of the Primal Substance. Depth under depth was the Dark Terror of the Abyss of Chaos. Before all things were the Waters of the Great Sea, wherein all the seeds of form lie.

Then from the Place of Dawn rose the Face of the Eternal, before Whose glorious Countenance the Terror of Darkness hasted away. In the Waters beneath was that Face reflected in the formless Abyss of the Void.

From those Eyes darted rays of terrible splendor, which crossed with the currents reflected. That Brow and those Eyes formed the triangle of the Measureless Waters. Thus was formulated the Eternal Hexad, the number of the Dawning Creation. (*Sits.*)

A-t: *Comes forward and, moving clockwise around the altar, leads Practicus eastward through the Pillars, around the temple, to the station of the EA. A-t hands the Cross of the Zodiac to the EA.*

Admission Badge

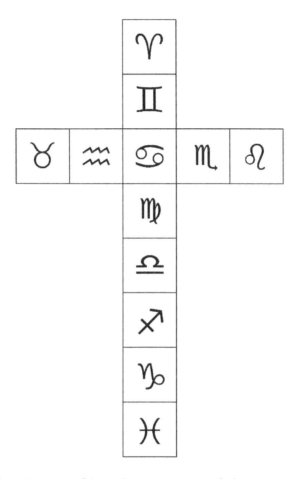

EA: The Cross of Twelve Squares fitly represents the zodiac, which embraces the Waters above the Firmament. It alludes to the Eternal River of Eden, divided into four heads, which find their correlations in the four triplicities of the Zodiac.

(*Places Cross aside.*)

CORPORAL INTELLIGENCE – Qoph

EA: The Twenty-ninth Path of the Sepher Yetzirah is called the Corporeal Intelligence, answering to the letter Qoph (ק). It is so-called because it marks out the forms of all bodies incorporated under every revolution of the Zodiac and constitutes the arrangement and the disposition thereof.

This is also the reflection of the watery sign Pisces. It is the path connecting the material universe, manifest in Malkuth, with the Pillar of Mercy and the side of Chesed, through the Sephirah Netzach. Through it, the waters of Chesed flow down to take form in the field of sensation as the material bodies of that sphere.

Leads A-t and Practicus to the West of the Altar, facing it.

EA: Before you on the altar is the Eighteenth Key of Tarot, symbolically resumes these ideas. It represents the Moon, with eighteen Hebrew Yods falling like dew drops. A dog and a wolf, two towers, a path leading to a height in the distance, and in the foreground, water with a crayfish crawling through it to the land completes the symbolism.

The Moon is in its increase on the side of Mercy. From it proceed sixteen principal and sixteen secondary rays, making 32 the number of the Paths of Wisdom.

The battlemented towers are symbols of the contending, warring forces presented to our minds by the appearances of the sphere of sensation.

Beyond them leads a path, rising to the heights of spiritual attainment and realization, the Mystic Mountain of our ancient Brethren of the Rosy Cross.

It is guarded by a wolf and a dog. Both are members of the same genus. Both are symbols of the desire-nature, which is the special task of the Philosophus to use and direct in his/her progress toward the goal of the Highest Good.

Rising from the pool, the crayfish refers to the truth that the operation of the Corporeal Intelligence has its first manifestations in forms whose natural habitat is water. By some, this crayfish is associated with the ancient god of Egypt, Khephra, a symbol of the Sun below the horizon, as he ever is when the Moon is increasing above.

Careful inspection of this Key will show the Philosophus that its symbolism is based on the ancient Qabalistic aphorism: "First the stone, then the plant, then the animal and then the man." All these are shown in the part of the design on the near side of the towers. Beyond them, the path leads to "more than man," the true Stone of the Wise. (*Returns to their station.*)

A-t: *Remains with Practicus, West of Altar.*

TITLE

EA: I have now much pleasure in conferring upon you the title of (Lord/Lady) of the Twenty-ninth Path. You will now quit the temple for a short time, and on your return, the ceremony of your passage through the Twenty-eighth Path will take place.

A-t: *Conducts Practicus out.*

END OF 1st POINT

GRADE OF PHILOSOPHUS

ARRANGEMENT FOR THE 2ND POINT

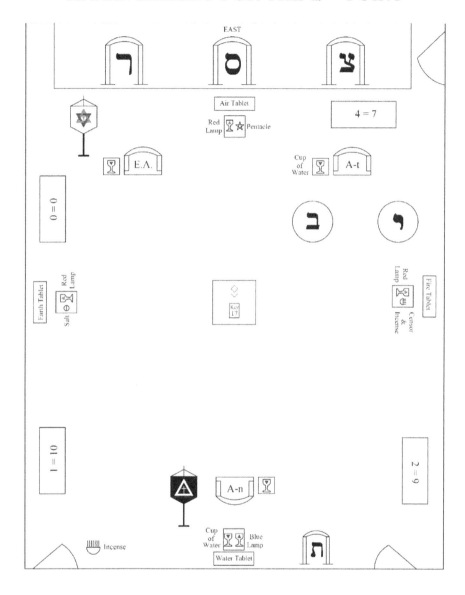

CHANGES FOR 2ND POINT

PORTALS

Change Eastern portals to Resh (Northeast), Samekh (East), and Tzaddi (Southeast). Place Tav in West.

ALTAR

Key 17 and Green Cube of Balanced Forces

These are the only changes.

PILLARS

The pillars remain the same place as the first point - southeast, facing east, black to the north.

Winged disk (see Appendix 6) with the letter Tzaddi (צ) between the pillars.

2nd POINT

EA: (Frater/Soror) A-t, you have my command to present the Practicus with the necessary Admission Badge and admit (him/her).

A-t: *Takes cube from the altar, leaves the temple and gives cube to Practicus, saying:*

This is the Cube of Balanced Forces. It is your Admission Badge into the Path of Aquarius, the Natural Intelligence.

Leads Practicus to Portal, admits him/her and says:

And ever forth from their Celestial Source, the Rivers of Eden flow.

(*Leads Practicus to Southeast before the Pillars. Points out Tzaddi on wings, as the EA mentions in the following speech.*)

28th PATH

EA: (Frater/Soror) Monoceros/Monocera de Astris, the Path open to you is the Twenty-eighth, leading from the Grade of Theoricus to that of Philosophus. Take the Cube of Balanced Forces in your right hand and follow your guide through the Path of the Water-Bearer.

A-t: *Leads Practicus through pillars and circumambulates the Temple 1 1/2 times with the Sun. Halts and faces the EA the second time they come to his/her station.*

RAIN

EA: *Rises as they approach, holding Cup.*

I am the rain of heaven, descending upon the earth, bearing the fructifying and germinating power with it. I am the plenteous yielder of harvest. I am the cherisher of Life. *(Sits.)*

A-t: *Leads Practicus to the station of A-n, halts and faces him/her.*

DEW

A-n: *Rises with Cup in hand*

I am the dew descending, invisible and silent, gemming the earth with countless diamonds of moisture, bearing down the influence from above in the solemn darkness of night. *(Sits.)*

MIST AND CLOUD

A-t: *Leads Practicus to own station, picks up Cup and says:*

I am the ruler of mist and cloud, wrapping the earth, as it were, in a garment, floating and hovering between earth and heaven. I am the giver of the mist-veil of autumn, the successor of the dew-clad night.

A-t: *Replaces Cup and leads Practicus to the West of the Altar, facing the EA. Returns to station and sits.*

EA: The Monad first existed, and the Paternal Monad still subsists. When the Monad is extended, the Dyad is generated and sits beside the Monad. This Dyad glitters with intellectual sections, through which it governs all things and sets in order everything not ordered. This order is the beginning of all sections.

A-n: In each world shineth the Triad, over which the Monad ruleth. The Mind of the Father said, "Into three," governing all things by mind. His Will assented, and immediately all things were so divided. All things are supplied from the bosom of this Triad. All things are governed and subsist in this Triad. And in the Triad appeared virtue and wisdom and multiscient truth.

A-t: From the Monad and Dyad floweth forth the form of the Triad, being pre-existent; not the first essence, but that whereby all things are measured. For thou must know that all things bow before the Three Supernals. They are the guardians of the works of the Father and the One Mind, the Intelligible.

Conducts Practicus through the pillars around the temple to stand before the EA. Hands EA the Cube of Balanced Forces.

Admission Badge

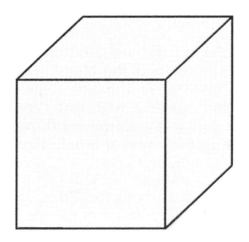

EA: The Admission Badge of this Path is the Cube of Balanced Forces. It is a symbol of the Divine Name, Yod Heh Vav Heh, because it has six faces, eight corners and twelve boundaries so that the sum of the numbers required to define its proportions is 26, the number of the Name, Yod Heh Vav Heh.

Because every face of a cube is equal to any of the other faces so that any one of the six sides may serve as its base, the cube has been, from time immemorial, a symbol of truth.

This truth unveils itself to man during meditation; thus, the cube is directly related to the meanings of the Twenty-eighth Path.

(*Put Cube aside.*)

NATURAL INTELLIGENCE

EA: The Twenty-eighth path of the Sepher Yetzirah, answering to the letter Tzaddi (צ), is called the Natural Intelligence. By it is perfected the nature of all things under the orb of the Sun. It is the reflection of the airy sign Aquarius, the Water-bearer. This sign is attributed to the Countenance of Man, the Adam who restores the world.

Leads A-t and Practicus to the West of the Altar, facing it.

EA: The Seventeenth Key of Tarot before you on the altar symbolically resumes these ideas.

The large star in the heavens has eight principal and eight secondary rays. This represents the Ogdoad multiplied by the Dyad and yields the number 16. This is the value of the Hebrew verb, Havaw (הוה), signifying primarily "to breathe." Thus, it is one of many symbols of the Cosmic Life-breath and the element of Air to which the Twenty-eighth Path is assigned.

Note that the three letters of "Havaw" are Heh, Vav and Heh, constituting the final portion of the Divine Name, Yod Heh Vav Heh, separated from the Paternal Yod. Thus the word represents the whole Tree of Life below Chokmah. The first Heh corresponds to Binah; the Vav represents the six Sephiroth constituting the Lesser Countenance; and the final Heh answers unto Malkuth.

The relation of this word to the great star in Key 17 establishes the latter as a symbol of all the powers of manifested existence, represented on the Tree of Life by the eight Sephiroth from Binah to Malkuth, inclusive.

Surrounding the large star are seven smaller stars. Each has eight points to show that each is of the same essential nature as the larger one. These seven are the seven "interior stars," corresponding to the seven alchemical metals and the seven Sephiroth from Binah to Yesod, inclusive.

The nude figure is the unveiled Isis or Venus-Urania. Thus, she is the power that dominates the Seventh Sephirah's activities, corresponding to the Grade of Philosophus. She is also Aima, Binah, Tebunah, the Great Supernal Mother, Aima Elohim, pouring the waters of creation upon the earth.

The two urns contain influences from Chokmah and Binah. That in her right hand stirs into activity the powers of the Ninth Sephirah, Yesod, represented by the pool. That in her left-hand divides itself into five streams, typifying the Quintessence, the four elements, and the subtle principles of sensation.

The bird of Hermes, lighting on the tree on her right, symbolizes the powers of Hod, the Eighth Sephirah. As a symbol of Venus, the kneeling woman corresponds to the powers operative in the Seventh Sephirah, and she is therefore placed to the right of the center of the design.

The mountain in the background symbolizes the Great Work and the Mystic Mountain of our ancient Brethren of the Rosy Cross.

(*Returns to his/her station and stands facing Practicus.*)

TITLE

EA: I have much pleasure in conferring upon you the title of (Lord/Lady) of the Twenty-eighth Path. You will now quit the temple for a short time, and on your return, the ceremony of your passage of the Twenty-seventh Path will take place.

A-t: *Leads Practicus out.*

END OF 2ND POINT

292

GRADE OF PHILOSOPHUS

ARRANGEMENT FOR THE 3RD POINT

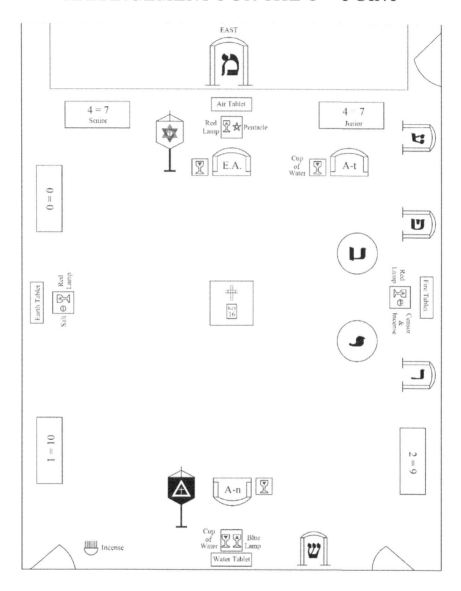

CHANGES FOR THE 3RD POINT

PORTALS

Mem in the east. Ayin in the southeast. Peh, just east of Fire Tablet. Resh in the southwest. Shin in the southwest or the right side of the A-n.

ALTAR

Cross of 10 Squares. Key 16.

PILLARS

Pillars facing south, before Fire Tablet (see below). The black pillar Boaz (ב) to the east.

Winged disk (see Appendix 6) with the letter Peh (פ) between the pillars.

OFFICERS

All officers in the east, facing west:
A-n is in the northeast.
EA is in the east.
A-t is in the southeast.

The red lamp replaces the cup on each officer's pedestal.

BANNERS

Banner of East, northeast of EA.

Banner of West, northeast of A-n.

3RD POINT

EA: (Frater/Soror) A-t, you have my command to present the Practicus with the necessary Admission Badge and admit (him/her).

A-t: *Goes out, gives Cross of 10 Squares to Practicus and says:*

This is the Cross of Ten Squares. It is your admission badge to the Path of Mars, the Exciting Intelligence.

Leads Practicus to the temple and admits him/her, halting just within the door. Says:

The river Kishon swept them away, that ancient river Kishon. O, my soul, thou hast trodden down strength.

Leads Practicus towards the south and places him/her in front of the Pillars on the north side of Pillars, facing south.

27th PATH OF PEH

EA: *

(Frater/Soror) Monoceros/Monocera de Astris, the Path now open to you is the Twenty-seventh, leading from Practicus to the Grade of Philosophus. Take in your right hand the Cross of the Sephiroth, and follow your guide through the Path of Mars.

A-t: The Lord is a man of war. Lord of Armies is His name.

KINGS OF EDOM

A-t leads Practicus between Pillars and around to EA following the Sun. They halt, facing the EA.

EA: (*rises; red lamp in hand.*)

Ere the Eternal instituted formation, beginning and end existed not. Therefore, He expanded a certain Veil before Him and instituted the Primal Kings. These kings reigned in Edom before a king reigned over Israel.

But they subsisted not. When the earth was formless and void - behold, this is the reign of Edom. And when Creation was established, lo, this is the reign of Israel. And the wars of titanic forces in the chaos of creation - these are the wars between them.

From a Light-bearer of insupportable brightness proceeded a radiant flame, hurling forth, like a vast and mighty hammer, those sparks which were the primal worlds. These sparks flamed and scintillated awhile, but being unbalanced, they were extinguished. Since, lo, the kings assembled, they passed away altogether. They beheld themselves, so they were astonished. They feared. They hasted away. These are the Kings of Edom, who reigned before there reigned a King in Israel. *(Sits.)*

A-t: *Takes Practicus around the temple and halts before A-n.*

A-n: *Rises with red lamp in hand.*

The Dukes of Edom were amazed. Trembling, they took hold of mighty Moab. The river Kishon swept them away, that ancient river Kishon. O, my soul, thou hast trodden down strength.

Lord, when Thou went out of Seir and marked out of the field of Edom, the earth trembled, and the heavens dropped; the clouds also dropped water.

He bowed the heavens and came down; the darkness was under His feet. At the brightness before Him, the thick clouds passed hailstones and flashings of fire. He sent forth His arrows and scattered them; He hurled forth his lightnings and destroyed them.

Then the channels of the waters were seen, and the foundations of the world were discovered. At Thy rebuke, O Lord, at the blast of the breath of Thy nostrils, the voice of Thy thunder was in the heavens, and Thy lightnings lightened the world. The earth trembled and shook. Thy way is in the sea, thy path in the great waters, and thy footsteps are unknown. *(Sits.)*

A-t: *Leads Practicus to his/her own station, lifts red lamp and says:*

O Lord, I have heard Thy speech and was afraid. The Voice of the Lord is upon the waters. The God of Glory thundered. The Lord is upon many waters. The Voice of the Lord is powerful. The Voice of the Lord is full of majesty. The Voice of the Lord breaketh the cedars of Lebanon. The Voice of the Lord divideth the flames of fire. The Voice of the Lord shaketh the wilderness of Kadesh.

Leads Practicus to the North of the Pillars, through them, then around the temple to the EA. Takes Cross from Practicus and gives it to EA.

ADMISSION BADGE

		1 כתר		
3 בינה	**5** גבורה	**6** תפארת	**4** חסד	**2** חכמה
		7 נצח		
		8 הוד		
		9 יסוד		
		10 מלכות		

EA: The Cross of Ten Squares refers to the Ten Sephiroth in balance disposition, before which the formless and void rolled back. It is also the opened-out form of the double cube and the altar of incense. (*Places the Cross aside.*)

EXCITING INTELLIGENCE

EA: The Twenty-seventh Path of the Sepher Yetzirah, answering unto Peh, is called the Exciting or Active Intelligence. It is so-called because thence is created the spirit of every creature under the supreme orb and the assemblage of them all.

It is also the reflection of the Sphere of Mars and the reciprocal path connecting Netzach with Hod, Victory with Splendor. This is the lowermost of the three reciprocal paths.

Leads A-t and Practicus to the West of the Altar, facing it.

KEY 16 – THE TOWER

EA: Before you on the altar is the Sixteenth Key of Tarot, symbolically resumes these ideas.

It represents a tower struck by lightning, issuing from a rayed circle and terminating in a triangle. This flash represents the Flaming Sword, as explained in a preceding Grade. Note that the circle and the flash resemble the astronomical symbol for Mars.

The tower refers to the Tower of Babel. It is built of twenty-two courses of brick, representing the elements of human speech when that speech is based upon the delusion of separateness, symbolized by the lonely peak on which the tower is erected.

The scene is one of a storm, corresponding to the ideas outlined in the speeches of the three Chief Officers you have just listened to. This symbolic language reveals ignorance and confusion that precedes truth's revelation. Herein is the occult meaning of the ancient Qabalistic doctrine concerning the Kings of Edom.

Three holes are rent in the tower's walls, symbolizing the Triad establishment therein.

On the right of the picture are ten Hebrew Yods arranged in the form of the Tree of Life diagram. They represent the powers of the inclusive Hebrew letters from Aleph to Yod. On the other side of the tower are twelve Hebrew Yods, so arranged that they suggest the outline of Figure 8 or Ogdoad. They represent the Hebrew letters from Kaph to Tav, inclusive.

Note that these twenty-two Yods hang, as it were, in the air. The purport of this is that the essential powers of Being represented by the Hebrew letters are self-supporting or without any material foundation other than themselves.

(*Returns to the throne.*)

A-t: *Remains with Practicus, West of Altar.*

TITLE

EA: I have much pleasure in conferring upon you the title of (Lord/Lady) of the Twenty-seventh Path. You will now quit the temple for a short time, and on your return, the ceremony of your admission to the Grade of Philosophus will take place.

A-t: *Leads Practicus out.*

END OF 3RD POINT

GRADE OF PHILOSOPHUS

ARRANGEMENT FOR THE 4TH POINT

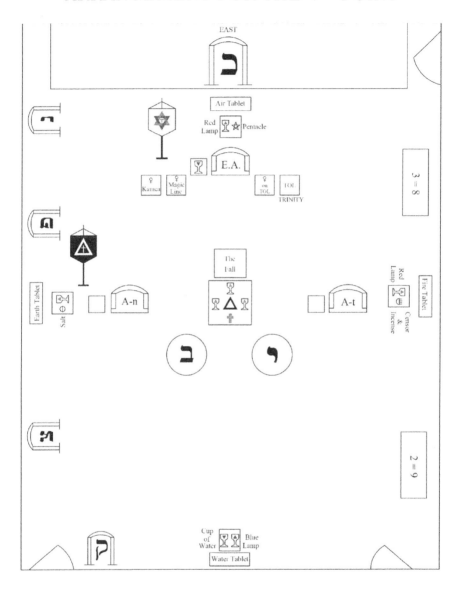

CHANGES FOR THE 4TH POINT

PORTALS

Kaph in the east. Qoph in the west, north of Water Tablet. Tzaddi in the northwest, west of Earth Tablet. Peh in the North, just east of Earth Tablet. Nun in the northeast.

ALTAR

Green Altar cloth covers Elemental Altar cloth. The triangle above the red calvary cross forms the Sulphur sign with 3 red candles at the triangle's points. East of the altar is the Diagram of the Fall.

OFFICERS

EA in the east. A-n south of Earth Tablet, facing west. A-t north of Fire Tablet.

Red lamps were removed from Officers' stations.

PILLARS

West of the Altar, facing east, as shown.

Remove the winged disk.

DIAGRAMS

Altar diagram. Four diagrams form a line west of EA's throne: Kamea of Venus, Magic Line of Venus, Venus on the Tree of Life, and Trinity on the Tree of Life.

GRADE OF PHILOSOPHUS

EA: (Frater/Soror) A-t, you have my command to present the Practicus with the necessary Admission Badge and to admit (him/her) upon (his/her) giving the proper alarm.

A-t: *Takes the Calvary Cross from the Altar, takes it to Practicus and says:*

This is the Red Calvary Cross. It is your admission badge to the Temple of Netzach.

Instructs him/her to knock ***** * ***** *and enter the temple alone, closing the door. After the Practicus has given the proper alarm, A-t admits him/her and closes the door. Points out Portals as EA names them.*

EA: The Portals of the Twenty-ninth and Twenty-eighth Paths are in the northwest. You have symbolically entered this grade from the Zelator and Theoricus Grades, respectively, while in the north is the portal of the Twenty-seventh Path by which you have just passed from the Grade of Practicus.

A-t: *Leads Practicus to A-n.*

A-n: By what symbol dost thou enter here?

A-t: By the Red Calvary Cross of six squares.

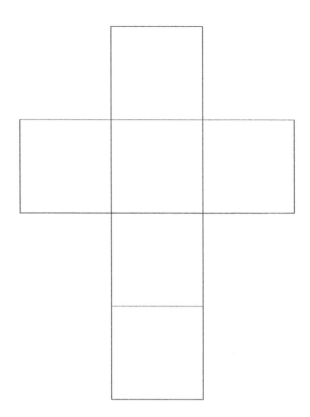

A-n: This Cross, already familiar to you, also represents the Sephiroth Tiphareth, Netzach, Hod and Yesod, resting upon Malkuth. This cross is also the pattern of the cube and is thus referred to as the sixth Sephiroth of the Microprosopus and to the balance of cosmic forces.

A-t: *Leads Practicus to the West of the Altar, facing east, and replaces the cross on the altar. Stands East of the Altar to point out details of the Diagram of the Fall.*

EA: *Comes to the west of the altar to explain the diagram.*

THE FALL DIAGRAM

EA: This is the symbolic representation of the Fall. For the Great Goddess, who in the Grade of Practicus was supporting the columns of the Sephiroth, in the sign of the Grade of Theoricus, being tempted by the Tree of Knowledge (whose branches, indeed, tend upward into the seven lower Sephiroth but also tend downward into the Kingdom of Shells), reached down unto the Qlippoth. Immediately the columns were unsupported, and the Sephirotic System was shattered, and with it fell Adam, the Microprosopus or Lesser Countenance.

Then arose the great Dragon with seven heads and ten horns, and the Garden was made desolate, and Malkuth was cut off from the Sephiroth by his intersecting folds and linked unto the Kingdom of the Shells. And the seven lower Sephiroth were cut off from the Three Supernals in Da'ath, at the feet of Aima Elohim.

And because in Da'ath was the greatest rise of the great Serpent of Evil, therefore is there, as it were, another Sephirah, making for the infernal or averse Sephiroth eleven instead of ten. And Da'ath, having developed in the Dragon a new head, the Seven-headed Dragon with ten horns became eight-headed and eleven-horned.

Hence were the rivers of Eden desecrated, and from the mouth of the Dragon rushed the infernal waters in Da'ath. And this is Leviathan, the crooked serpent.

But between the devastated Garden and the Supernal Eden, Yod Heh Vav Heh Elohim placed the letters of the name, and the Flaming Sword, that the uppermost part of the Tree of Life might not be involved in the Fall of Adam. And thence it was necessary that the Second Adam should come to restore all things, and that, as the First Adam had been extended on the Cross of the Celestial Rivers, the Son should be crucified on the Cross of the Infernal Rivers of Da'ath. Yet, to do this, he must descend unto the lowest first, even unto Malkuth.

SIGNS AND TOKENS OF PHILOSOPHUS

EA: The Grade of Philosophus is referred unto the
Sephirah Netzach, and the Twenty-seventh,
Twenty-eighth and Twenty-ninth Paths are
bound to it.

The sign of the grade is given by raising the hands
to the forehead and with the thumbs and index
fingers forming a triangle, apex up, thus, . . . This
represents the element of Fire to which this grade
is allotted and the spirit that moved upon the
Waters of Creation.

The grip or token is the general grip of the First
Order. The Grand Word is a Name of nine letters:
Yod Heh Vav Heh Tzabaoth, (צבאות יהוה) which
means "Lord of Armies."

The Mystic Number is 28, and the password is
formed: Kaph, Cheth; Kach (כח). It should be
lettered separately when given, with the one who
gives the password saying the first letter, the one
who receives it saying the second, and the one
who gives it saying the word: Kach. It means
power.

OCCULT OR HIDDEN INTELLIGENCE

EA: Unto this Grade, and unto the Sephirah Netzach, the Seventh Path of the Sepher Yetzirah is referred. It is called the Occult or Hidden Intelligence, and it is so-called because it is the brilliant splendor of all the intellectual powers that are beheld by the eye of understanding and the thought of faith.

BALDRIC OF PRACTICUS

The distinguishing badge of this grade, which you will now be entitled to wear, is the baldric of a Practicus, with the addition of a green cross above the orange cross and the numbers 4 in a circle and 7 in a square on either side; and below the number 30, the numbers 29, 28 and 27 in red-violet, violet and red, respectively, between narrow white bars.

FIRE TABLET

ל	ו	ר	כ	י	א	ל	מ	י	כ	א	ל
ע	י	ו	ה	ר	י	נ	ס	ט	נ	ד	ר
ח	פ	ע	ט	א	ו	י	ז	ל	ב	ר	א
ז	ס	ה	י	א	ל	ש	ר	ט	י	ה	ב
י	ז	ר	ה	ב	נ	י	מ	י	א	י	ו
מ	ו	ש	ד	ט	ל	ה	א	נ	ל	ת	ה
ה	ה	ל	ו	ל	ש	ש	ר	א	ס	ל	א
ה	א	א	ה	א	א	ר	י	י	ר	ב	מ
ב	מ	ס	י	ר	א	פ	ה	א	י	ר	ל
ת	ה	ע	ד	ג	ת	ש	ק	ל	ט	מ	כ
א	נ	י	ו	ס	ל	א	ו	ע	י	י	י
ר	ס	נ	ט	ע	ר	ט	ס	ל	א	מ	ד
ש	מ	ר	ה	נ	ס	ו	ל	ר	ז	ז	א

This grade is specially referred to as Fire, and therefore, the Great Watchtower or Terrestrial Tablet of the South forms one of its principal emblems. It is known as the Fourth or Great Southern Quadrangle and is one of the four great Tablets of the Elements. From it are drawn the three holy, secret names of God: Hehela, Valashishi, Reashila, borne upon the Banner of the South, and numberless Divine and Angelic Names which appertain to the element of Fire.

The triangle surmounting the cross upon the altar represents the Fire of Spirit, surmounting the Cross of Life, and also the cross of the waters of Edom.[6] You will note that thus it forms the alchemical emblem of Sulphur. The red lamps at the triangle angles are the three-fold form of Fire.

The portals in the East and Northeast conduct higher Grades. The others are those Paths you have already traversed.

(*Resumes his/her throne.*)

כב	זמ	יו	אמ	י	הל	ד
ה	גכ	חמ	יז	מב	אי	טכ
ל	ו	דכ	טמ	יח	ול	בי
גי	אל	ז	הכ	גמ	טי	זל
חל	די	בל	א	וכ	דמ	כ
אכ	טל	ח	לג	ב	זכ	המ
ומ	וט	מ	ט	דל	ג	חכ

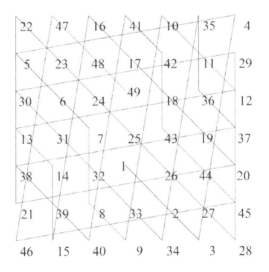

A-t: *Conducts Practicus to Kamea of Venus.*

The Grade of Philosophus is attributed to the Sphere of Venus, which is ruler in Netzach, and therefore the Kamea, or Magic Square, of Venus and the Magic Line formed therefrom are among its emblems. Moreover, from it are drawn the sigils relating to the planet Venus, together with Divine and Angelic Names pertaining to that planet.

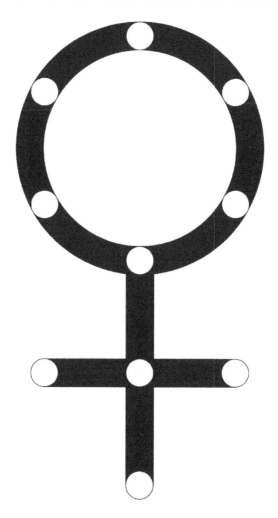

A-t: *Conducts Practicus to Venus on the Tree.*

The symbol of Venus, inscribed on the Tree of Life, is shown in the diagram before you. It embraces the whole of the Sephiroth and is, therefore, a fitting emblem of the Isis of Nature; hence, its circle is larger than Mercury's.

TRINITY ON THE TREE OF LIFE

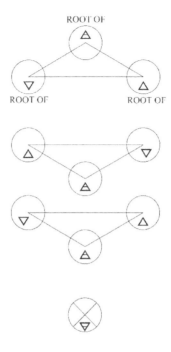

A-t: (*Conducts Practicus to Trinity on the Tree.*)

This diagram refers to the Trinity or the "Three Mothers" operating through the Sephiroth and reflected downward in the four triangles of the elements. Kether is the Root of Air, reflected downward from Kether to Yesod through Tiphareth. Chokmah is the Root of Fire, reflected from Chokmah, through Geburah, to Netzach. Binah is the Root of Water, which is reflected from Binah, through Chesed, to Hod.

The tenth Sephirah Malkuth is Earth, the receptacle and synthesis of Air, Fire and Water.

(*Leads Practicus to face EA.*)

MYSTIC TITLE

EA: I now congratulate you on having passed through the ceremony of the Grade of Philosophus, and in recognition thereof, I confer upon you the Mystic Title of Pharos Illuminans, which means "Illuminating Tower of Light," and I give you the symbol of Esh (אש), which is the Hebrew name for Fire.

And, as having attained at length to the highest Grade of the First Order, and being, as it were, a connecting link with the Second Order, I further confer upon you the title of respect, "Honored (Frater/Soror)," and I give you the further symbol of Phrath, or the Euphrates, the Fourth River.

PROCLAMATION

EA: *

In the name of **YOD HEH VAV HEH TZABAOTH**, I now proclaim that you have been duly advanced to the Grade of Philosophus and that you are (Lord/Lady) of the Twenty-seventh, Twenty-eighth and Twenty-ninth Paths.

A-t: (*Leads Philosophus to A-n's throne.*)

A-N's ADDRESS

A-n: Honored (Frater/Soror), as a member of this important grade, you are eligible for the post of A-n when a vacancy occurs. You are furthermore expected, having risen so high in the Order, to aid to your utmost the members of the Second Order in the Working of the Temple to which you are attached; to study thoroughly the mysteries which have been unfolded to your view in your progress from the humble position of Neophyte, so that yours may not be the merely superficial knowledge which marks the conceited and ignorant person; but that you may really and thoroughly understand what you profess to know, and not by your ignorance and folly bring disgrace on that Order which has honored you so far. Your duty is also to supervise the studies of weaker and less advanced brethren and make yourself, as far as possible, an ornament like your Lodge and the Order.

A-t: *Conducts new Philosophus to a seat of a 4=7, in the extreme southeast in front of the dais, facing west. Returns to own station and sits.*

END OF ATTUNEMENT

CLOSING

All: *(Standing at their places.)*

EA: * Fratres et Sorores of the *(name of organization)*
_____, assist me in closing _____ Lodge,
Number _____, in the Grade of Philosophus.
(Frater/Soror) A-t, see that the Temple is properly
guarded.

A-t: *Give Grade sign, checks doors, return to the
station, then:*

* Very Honored EA, the temple is properly
guarded.

EA: * * * Let us adore the Lord and King of Fire.

All: All *face south.*

ADORATION

EA: **YOD HEH VAV HEH TZABAOTH,** Mighty and
Terrible! Commander of the ethereal armies, art
Thou!

All: **AMEN.** *(All give the sign of the grade.)*

PRAYER OF THE SALAMANDERS

All: *EA goes to the south before the Tablet of Fire. A-n stands behind and to the right of EA. A-t places the new Philosophus behind EA and goes to a position behind and to the left of the EA. Thus the three officers form a triangle with the Philosophus in the center. Other Philosophi arranges themselves in balanced formation behind A-n and A-t.*

(Fire Tablet in the South)

EA

A-t   Phil   A-n

H-r

C-n   P-r

EA: Let us rehearse the Prayer of the Salamanders or Fire Spirits.

* Immortal, eternal, ineffable and uncreated Father of all things, Who art borne upon the ever-rolling chariot of worlds which revolve without cessation; Ruler of the ethereal immensities where the throne of Thy power is exalted, from which summit Thy terrible eyes behold all things, and Thy pure and holy ears harken unto all - - Hear us, Thy children, who Thou hast loved since before the birth of the Ages! Thy Majesty, golden, vast and eternal, shineth above the world and the heaven of stars. Over them, all art Thou exalted, O Thou Glittering Fire!

There dost Thou commune with Thyself by Thine own splendor; endless streams of Light pour from thine essence for the nourishment of Thine infinite spirit. This spirit Itself doth nourish all things and formeth an inexhaustible treasure of substance, ever ready for generation, adapting and appropriating the forms Thou hast impressed on it from the beginning.

From this spirit arise the three most holy Kings who surround Thy throne and constitute Thy court.

O Universal Father, One and Alone, Father alike of immortals and mortals! Thou hast specially created powers like unto Thine eternal Thought and one with Thy venerable essence. Thou hast established them above the angels who proclaim Thy Will to the world. Finally, Thou hast created us, third in rank within our elemental empire.

There our continual exercise is to praise Thee and adore Thy good pleasure; there, we burn continually with eternal aspiration unto Thee. O, Father! O Mother, most tender of all Mothers! O archetype eternal of maternity and of pure love! O Son, the flower of all sons! O form of all forms! Soul, Spirit, Harmony and Numberer of all things!

All: **AMEN.**

LICENSE TO DEPART - Salamanders

EA: *Makes the following figures before the Tablet of Fire:*

EA: Depart ye in peace unto your habitations. May the blessing of YOD HEH VAV HEH TZABAOTH be upon ye! Be there peace between you and us, and be ye ready to come when ye are called. * (*EA veils Fire Tablet.*)

All: *EA returns to the throne and veils the Air Tablet...*

A-t: *A-t conducts new Philosophus back to their seat, then veils Water Tablet.*

A-n: *Veils the Earth Tablet.*

All: *All return to their stations and places and sit.*

EA: Honored Frater/Soror _____, perform the Lesser Banishing Pentagram of Fire.

(*Designated member performs the Banishing Ritual.*)

CLOSING DECLARATION

EA: In the Name of **YOD HEH VAV HEH TZABAOTH**, I declare this temple closed in the Grade of Philosophus.

EA: *** * ***

A-n: *** * ***

A-t: *** * ***

0 = 0 CLOSING (SHORT FORM)

EA: Dispensing with all further ceremony, I now declare this temple closed as a Hall of Neophytes of the (*name of organization*)_____.

EA: *

A-n: *

A-t: *

END OF CEREMONY

CHAPTER 4 NOTES

[1] TRACING THE EQUAL-ARMED CROSS

The cross is drawn with the lines traced on top of each
other. The lines are shown below with separation to
emphasize the directions – start in the center, trace
top to bottom, back to center, then right to the left.

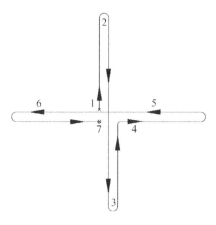

The Qabalah of the 9 Chambers										
Shin	Lamed	Gimel		Resh	Kaph	Beth		Qoph	Yod	Aleph
שׁ	ל	ג		ר	כ	ב		ק	י	א
300	30	3		200	20	2		100	10	1
Final Mem	Samekh	Vav		Final Kaph	Nun	Heh		Tau	Mem	Daleth
ם	ס	ו		ך	נ	ה		ת	מ	ד
600	60	6		500	50	5		400	40	4
Final Tzaddi	Tzaddi	Teth		Final Peh	Peh	Cheth		Final Nun	Ayin	Zain
ץ	צ	ט		ף	פ	ח		ן	ע	ז
900	90	9		800	80	8		700	70	7

³ IHVH in the FOUR WORLDS

Tetragrammaton in the Four Worlds					#
Qabalistic World	Yod י	Heh ה	Vav ו	Heh ה	26
Atziloth	יוד	הי	ויו	הי	72
Briah	יוד	הי	ואו	הי	63
Yetzirah	יוד	הא	ואו	הא	45
Assiah	יוד	הה	וו	הה	52

Derived from page 33 [plate 5] of Kabbalah Unveiled.

I found the image to the right online. However, if you compare it to the actual arrangement of the sephiroth, they don't line up.

I don't know if this was a mistake or a poetic arrangement of the sephiroth on the sulfur symbol.

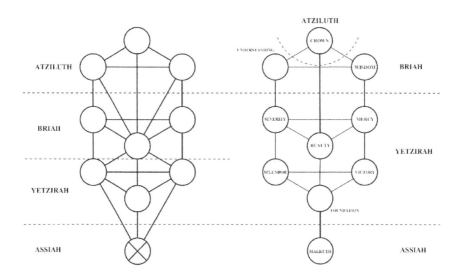

I've seen these two arrangements of the Tree of Life in the Four Worlds. Depending on perspective, both are valid.

^{6} EDEN vs. EDOM

The Golden Dawn ritual says "waters of Eden." The PFC ritual says, "Edom." I don't know if this is a typo or intended. I think it's a typo.

The 3 = 8 grade document is shown on the left.

The left image is like the one in the grade work. The right-hand drawing shows the sephiroth's actual arrangement overlayed on the Venus symbol.

I don't know if this was a mistake or a poetic arrangement of the sephiroth on the Venus symbol.

APPENDIX 1

RITUAL NOTES

Generally speaking, the candidate is ADMITTED into the lodge on the first point. Then, when the candidate has met the test, the last point the initiate is RECEIVED into the grade.

Generally, but not always, the candidate is raised or attuned to the next grade by the *Command* of the EA/Hierophant and the PROCLAMATION of the H-r/Kerux.

Usually, the candidate is tested for their knowledge in the first point. After that, the guardians meet along the *Paths* on the Tree of Life or the Inverse Tree, the *Tunnels* of Set. Finally, the candidate is admitted into the sephiroth corresponding to the grade at the last point. There they receive instruction.

At the end of each attunement, the element invoked in the opening is BANISHED. However, this term is too harsh, and I prefer the medieval magician's *License to Depart*.

TEMPLE LIGHTS

In the 3 = 8 ritual, the temple lights are dimmed for the 31st and 30th Paths. After the candidate meets the guardians, the initiate is led through the pillars, and the lights are turned up. Then, the candidate receives instruction.

I was told that dimming the lights symbolizes entering the astral realm. The lights restored to brightness symbolize returning to this plane to receive instruction.

However, these notes do not appear in the other three attunement rituals. Therefore, practicing this for the other paths seems like a good idea. However, I hesitate to make the change if there is a good reason the other rituals don't observe the same procedure.

ADORATION TO THE ELEMENTS

The ADORATION of the 1 = 10, 3 = 8 and 4 = 7 rituals begins with the EA facing the direct and tracing a circle in the air towards the element's direction.

I like to trace circles, starting and ending at the bottom. This formation builds and holds energy the best from my sense of touch. Otherwise, you can start the circle base on the elements' quadrant, as shown in Appendix 2.

PREPARING FOR A CEREMONY

Begin by reading your part aloud at least once daily, starting a month before the attunement. If you're sitting down when giving your speech, practice sitting down. Likewise, if you're standing for the ritual, say your part is standing. You think we are prepared for the ceremony, but the little things can trip us up.

For impact on the candidate, some parts of the ritual need to be memorized. For example, in the Zelator ritual, The Path of Evil:

> And the angel Samael answered and said: "I am the Prince of Darkness and Evil. The wicked and rebellious man gazeth upon the face of nature and findeth therein naught but terror and obscurity. It is but darkness of darkness to him, and he is as a drunken man groping in darkness. *Points to the direction they approached.*
> Return, for thou canst not pass by! *(Sits)*

I have Venus conjunct, my ascendant, so I enjoy acting. I stop shaving and washing my hair a few days before the ceremony. I roll my words like my basic training instructor and show off my missing tooth when I say my part. In fact, I practice making faces in front of a mirror. Your voice need not be loud to impress the candidate; rumbly and grumbly will do.

Try to recall, for a moment during a ritual, that you are impressing the Tree of Life into your subconscious mind. We are literally and figuratively building our immortal body. Also, the four attunement rituals are the purification and consecration of our elemental bodies. The rituals are an exercise in self-immolation, so never turn down an opportunity to be a part of an attunement ritual.

APPENDIX 2

Quadrants of a Circle and the Elements

Note that in the opening rituals' invocation (and banishing), the starting point quadrant for the circle is different for each ritual.

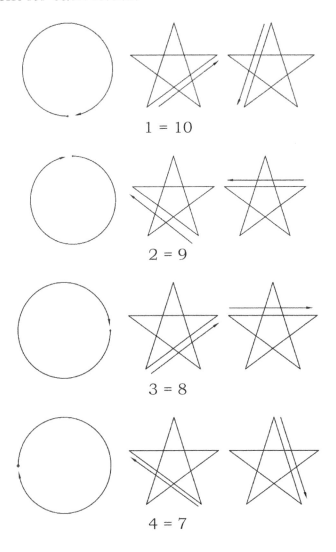

1 = 10

2 = 9

3 = 8

4 = 7

Merging the four drawings gives this figure.

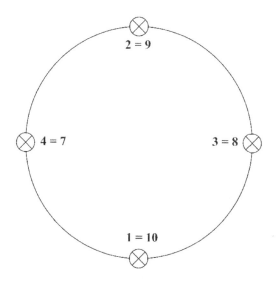

I'm not sure why we have this pattern. My first thought is to reverse the 4 = 7 and 3 = 7, so they are on the same side Tree of Life as their corresponding sphere. I'm sure there is a reason why it is what it is, but I don't know. Please contact me at the email at the back of the book if anyone knows.

APPENDIX 3

Mixing Acrylic Paints

Many diagrams in the grade work are made to be colored. If you use acrylic paints, these work well.

Red

Liquitex (tube) Naphthol Crimson, No. 1045-292 (or plastic bottle, No. 2002-292). Be sure to put on several coats for a deep color.

Red Orange

Liquitex (tube) Scarlet Red, (Cadmium Red Light Hue), No. 1045-510

Orange

Liquitex (tube) Indo Orange Red, No. 1045-242

Yellow-Orange

Liquitex (plastic bottle) Brilliant Orange, No. 2002-720 (mixed with a small amount of Yellow)

Yellow

Liquitex (plastic bottle) Yellow Medium Azo, No. 2002-412

Yellow Green

Liquitex (tube) Light Emerald Green, No. 1045-650

Green

Liquitex (tube) Permanent Green Deep, No. 1045-350

Blue Green

Americana (plastic bottle) Teal Green, No. DA107 and Americana True Blue, No. DA36 mixed half and half

Blue

Liquitex – "Basics" (plastic tube), Cobalt Blue Hue, No. 1046-170. Note: The Basics Cobalt gives a more accurate color than the bottle and is cheaper.

Blue Violet

Americana (plastic bottle) Prussian Blue No. DA138 and Americana Dioazine Purple, No. DA101 – mixed 1 part blue to 3 parts purple, then add a drop of white (Americana Titanium – Snow White, No. DA1)

Violet

Americana (plastic bottle) Dioxazine Purple, No. DA101, or Liquitex "Basics" (tube) Dioxazine Purple No. 1046-186 (This shade of Liquitex tends to get dark, go lightly or add a little white).

Red Violet

Liquitex (tube) Prism Violet, No. 1045-391, lightened with some white.

APPENDIX 4

INCENSE FOR RITUALS

For the neophyte and the 1 = 10 Zelator ritual, we used Dittany of Crete.

2 = 9 THEORICUS

Path of Tav (Saturn): The grade work lists Asafoetida and Scammony. Asafoetida is called Devil's Dung because of its foul smell and bitter taste. Scammony root is used as a laxative and as an antiparasitic. Using this incense, you will clear the temple with its choking fumes. In practice, we used Dittany of Crete for the Path of Tav.

The Path of Yesod (The Moon): Jasmine is the preferred incense.

3 = 8 PRACTICUS

Path of Shin (Root of Fire): Olibanum or Frankincense. The grade work says to use frankincense. It is the fiery elemental incense of Moses.

Path of Resh (The Sun): Also Frankincense.

The Path of Hod (Mercury): The grade work suggests and then dismisses the incense storax. The internet says storax has a pleasant, floral/lilac, leathery, balsamic smell. I have a blend from *Alchemy Works* website of white sandalwood, lavender and mastic cassia that I use for works of Mercury.

4 = 7 PHILOSOPHUS

The Path of Qoph (Pisces): The grade work list ambergris. Ambergris, French for grey amber, is generally called whale vomit. For those who object to animal products, the *Alchemy Works* website has a section, "Zodiacal Incense for Magical Work," with suitable plant substitutes for Pisces.

The Path of Tzaddi (Aquarius): The grade work lists galbanum. It has an intense green fragrance with woody and balsamic elements. The grade work says the green note gives it an airy quality. Galbanum is related to fennel and is mentioned in Exodus 30:34.

> "Then the Lord said to Moses, 'Take fragrant spices—gum resin, onycha and galbanum—and pure frankincense, all in equal amounts.'"

The Path of Peh (Mars); the grade work lists pepper, dragon's blood and all pungent odors (including tobacco). I like dragon's blood, a resin of a palm tree native to an archipelago in the Arabian Sea.

The Path of Netzach (Venus): The grade work lists rose, benzoin, myrtle and red sandalwood. Rose and red sandalwood are my favorites. Patchouli is good, and the scent reminds me of Grateful Dead concerts.

APPENDIX 5

TEMPLE FURNITURE

ALTAR CONSTRUCTION

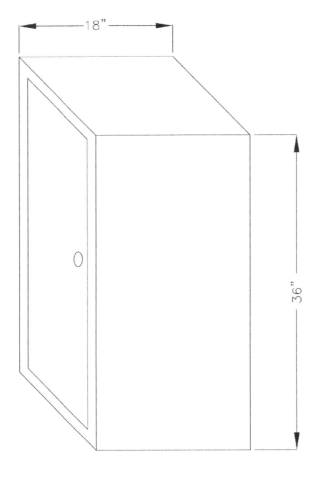

The altar is a double cube 36 inches tall. Castor wheels make moving the altar much easier.

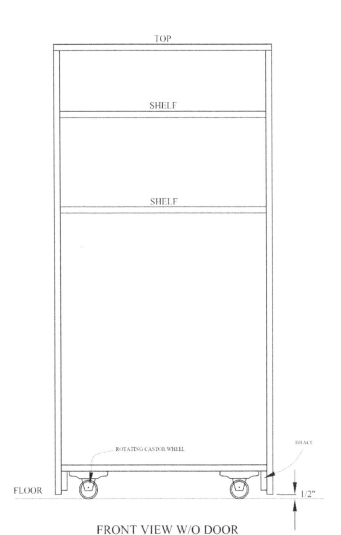

TOP

SHELF

SHELF

ROTATING CASTOR WHEEL

BRACE

FLOOR

1/2"

FRONT VIEW W/O DOOR

The half-inch height above the floor is a suggestion. This depends on the floor surface. If the temple is carpeted, more height may be necessary. And if it's a hardwood floor, less is needed.

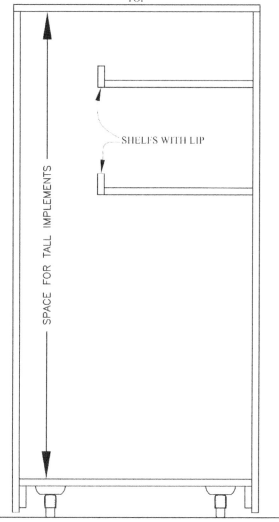

TOP

SPACE FOR TALL IMPLEMENTS

SHELFS WITH LIP

SIDE VIEW

On the top shelf is a place for drapes covering the officers' tables at their stations. The lip keeps them from spilling to the floor when the altar is moved. Carefully arranged, most temple furnishings and implements can be placed inside.

OFFICERS' SCEPTERS

The scepter handles are 18 inches long and turned on a lathe. Since they are used for striking with a firm hand to make knocks, they are best made of hardwood. Notice the bottom is rounded, making for a loud knock even if you strike at an odd angle. Three scepters are for the chiefs, and the other two are for the EA and A-t.

A suitable diameter is 1 to 1-1/4 inches because it fits well in hand.

Then purchase a 12" x 12 copper sheet that's 1/8" (11 gauge) to ¼" thick (3 gauge).

The shapes needed for the scepter tops are a circle, pentagram and hexagram.

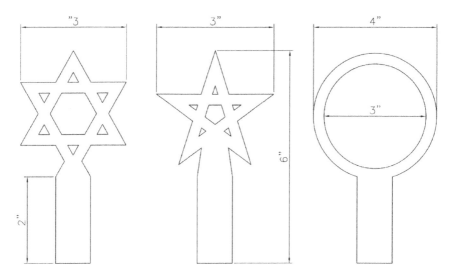

These figures fit on the 12" x 12" copper plate with careful placement.

Once the copper pieces are cut out, use a file to smooth the rough edges.

Then cut a 2" slot in the top of the wooden scepter handle. The width should allow the scepter tops to slide into place with a snug fit. But not too tight that it splits the wood.

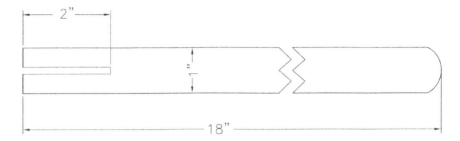

Turn the scepter 90 degrees and drill two holes.

Slide in the scepter top and use a pencil to mark the metal through the two holes. Next, remove the scepter top, place it on a flat surface and drill the two holes.

Slide the scepter back into place and use a nut and bolt to secure the scepter top in place. If you have carpentry skills, you can countersink the holes so the screws are flush with the surface of the wood. After construction, the scepters are painted the appropriate colors.

A-n SWORD

For the A-n sword, I don't recommend using a full-length sword. This is because it is held in a salute, and a long sword gets heavy.

I like a dagger with a 12" to 18" length.

Note the sturdy round bottom pommel for knocks.

The H'r's staff is typically 3 feet long. It's divided into three sections with a small raised band. On the staff ends are octahedrons. One end is blunt for rapping.

The other end has a rounded point. However, it is not as sharp as shown in the drawing below. This is because sharp points on wood have a tendency to chip.

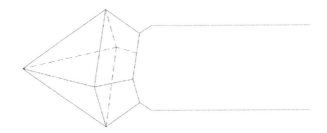

Turning the staff on a lathe with one piece of wood is best. Leave the ends shaped by the lathe but the finishing carved by hand into an octahedron.

You will be tempted to build the staff in sections, drill holes in the center and then hold it together with dowels. But, with the rapping and barring the staff endures, it is only a matter of time before it breaks.

CROSS and TRIANGLE

The grade work doesn't state the dimensions of the cross and triangle, so I traced our lodge implements on a page of my 1 = 10 grade work. I don't claim they are the "correct" dimensions, just the size our lodge used.

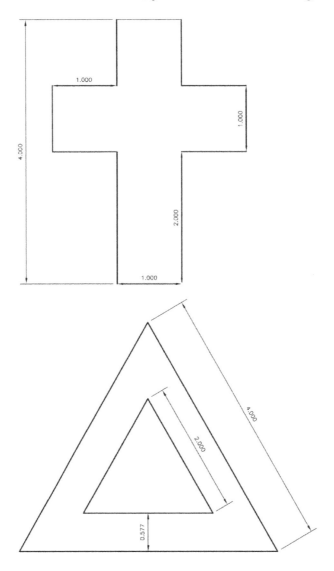

THE PILLARS

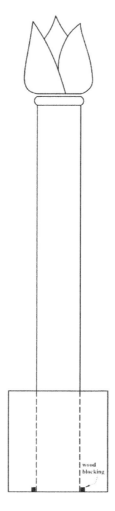

The tops are lotus buds. Our temple had them carved with a chainsaw and then painted. The lotus buds are heavy, so the columns were 10" diameter PVC pipe to hold them up. The half-inch plywood base was also weighty and wide to stabilize everything.

First, make the lotus capitals, then size the columns. In most hardware stores, you can find sonotubes (heavy-duty cardboard tubes used for construction.

Recall in the 3 = 8 ritual the placement of the pillars for the second point.

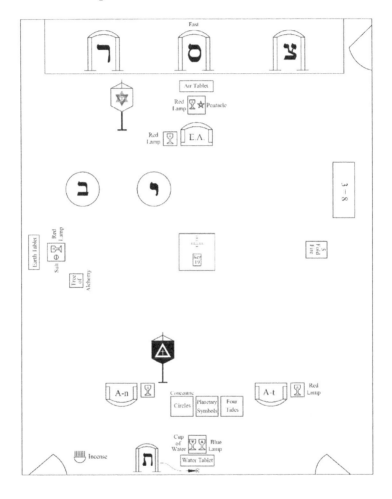

The pillars are wide enough for the candidate and their guide to walk between them with the winged disk above.

APPENDIX 6

WINGED DISK

Hung between the pillars is a pole (broomstick) that supports a winged figure with a Hebrew letter held in place by Velcro. For example, the candidate passes symbolically through a portal and enters the 30th Path of Resh.

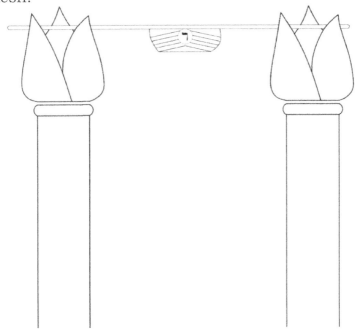

Therefore the height of the pillars should be at least six and a half feet. Otherwise, the taller candidates will need to duck under.

Generally, the temple lights are dim while the initiate meets the guardians. Then, the lights are raised when the candidate walks through the portal. I like to pause before the portal, point to the Hebrew letter, and walk through it with the candidate.

OBTW

Except for the Path of Tav (ת), all other paths (in the higher grades) are traversed with pillars wide enough for the candidate and the guide to pass through with a winged disk above.

PAUL FOSTER CASE BOOKS

1. SEVEN STEPS IN PRACTICAL OCCULTISM

2. AN INTRODUCTION TO THE TAROT AND ASTROLOGY

3. TAROT FUNDAMENTALS

4. TAROT INTERPRETATIONS

5. THE MASTER PATTERN

6. THE THIRTY-TWO PATHS OF WISDOM

7. THE TREE OF LIFE

8. THE NEOPHYTE RITUALS OF PAUL FOSTER CASE

9. THE ATTUNEMENT RITUALS OF PAUL FOSTER OF CASE

10. THE SECOND ORDER RITUALS OF PAUL FOSTER CASE

WADE COLEMAN BOOKS

1. SEPHER SAPPHIRES Volume 1

2. SEPHER SAPPHIRES Volume 2

3. THE ASTROLOGY WORKBOOK

4. MAGIC OF THE PLANETS

5. THE ZODIAC OF DENDARA EGYPT

6. THE MAGICAL PATH

7. ATHANASIUS KIRCHER'S QUADRIVIUM

To contact the author,

DENDARA_ZODIAC@protonmail.com

Made in the USA
Las Vegas, NV
13 September 2023

77509810R00197